ISBN 978-1-333-34513-6
PIBN 10493254

1 MONTH OF
FREE
READING

at
www.ForgottenBooks.com

By purchasing this book you are
eligible for one month membership to
ForgottenBooks.com, giving you
unlimited access to our entire
collection of over 700,000 titles via
our web site and mobile apps.

To claim your free month visit:

www.forgottenbooks.com/free493254

English
Français
Deutsche
Italiano
Español
Português

www.forgottenbooks.com

Mythology Photography **Fiction**
Fishing Christianity **Art** Cooking
Essays Buddhism Freemasonry
Medicine **Biology** Music **Ancient**
Egypt Evolution Carpentry Physics
Dance Geology **Mathematics** Fitness
Shakespeare **Folklore** Yoga Marketing
Confidence Immortality Biographies
Poetry **Psychology** Witchcraft
Electronics Chemistry History **Law**
Accounting **Philosophy** Anthropology
Alchemy Drama Quantum Mechanics
Atheism Sexual Health **Ancient History**
Entrepreneurship Languages Sport
Paleontology Needlework Islam
Metaphysics Investment Archaeology
Parenting Statistics Criminology
Motivational

DEDICATION.

—◆—

TO

COLONEL RICHARD ELLISON,

OF

SUDBROOK HOLME, LINCOLNSHIRE,

AND

MEMBER OF PARLIAMENT FOR WOTTON BASSET,

WILTSHIRE,

𝕿𝖍𝖎𝖘 𝖁𝖔𝖑𝖚𝖒𝖊,

WITH EVERY SENTIMENT OF RESPECT AND ESTEEM,

IS VERY GRATEFULLY INSCRIBED.

BY HIS OBLIGED AND OBEDIENT SERVANT,

CHARLES SWAN.

A 2

PREFACE.

A PREFACE to a Book is as naturally ex-
pected as a Book to a Preface; and on en-
tering a literary career, I should be exceed-
ingly loth to err in a matter *so* important!
Under this impression, therefore, I put my
hand to the oar.

The subject of the " Counterfeit Saints"
is, I am aware, a point of much nicety;
and in steering far away from the shores of
Superstition, we are perhaps too liable to
be foundered on the opposite coast: but,
dangerous as the pilotage may be, it is not
impracticable—and so far, I venture to be-
lieve, I have succeeded; at least, this I can
with safety aver—I have never designedly
intended to throw an air of ridicule over the
interests dearest to Religion! This asser-
tion seems the more necessary, since there
are in the world a sort of people, dull as
they are mischievous—reptiles, discovered
to have been, only by the slime they leave;
who turn the little wit with which Heaven
hath supplied them, to pervert the tendency
of every casual expression*; who hunt with

---

* What was said of the " Goths and Vandals" of a
former age, may with equal propriety be applied to the
barbarians of this! " Quicquid non placet, quicquid

A 3

the perseverance, but not with the sagacity of hounds, for a miserable subsistence, and who would have us imagine, that they are the best and warmest members of society, who bring the dark shades to light, and throw the light into obscurity; and who, like voracious truants, raise all the filth of the kennel, to gloat upon the refuse it contains! But the injury is not confined among themselves; some, and those too of sound judgment and candour, are carried down by the stream, (for the current of a *puddle* may sweep away the purest gold!) and to such only would I address myself. *They* will perhaps allow for the heat of youth, or at least, they will not convert the errors of the head, into the faults of the heart!

With regard to the remaining pieces—as they are less, so, doubtless, they are less faulty; however this may be, I can only wish them a safe conduct through this world of criticism, but without altogether concurring in the sentiment, that

" Whatever is, is *right!*"

C. S.

Askron, *Jan. 8th*, 1819.

---

non intelligunt, *Hæresis* est; Græcè scire Hæresis est; expolitè loqui Hæresis est; et quicquid sapsi non faciunt *Hæresis est.*—*Erasmi Epist. Basil.* 1521. *p.* 477.

Preface

THE SECOND EDITION.

———

THE unlooked-for and rapid sale of a large impression of the " COUNTERFEIT SAINTS," notwithstanding the impediments thrown out by the malevolence of some, and the ignorant conceit of others, has loudly called for a Second Edition. To reply to every objection which has been, or may be, started against this, or the Poems following, would be an useless, if not an impossible task. I shall, however, beg leave to transcribe for their perusal, a story from Boccalini, which affords a sufficient reproof (sufficient for me at least) to all the would-be wits and critics who have done me the honour to notice my *entré* into the literary world—leaving them to apply it as they think good!—" A famous Critic having gathered together all the faults of an eminent Poet, made a present of them to Apollo, who received them very graciously, and resolved to make the Author a suitable return for the trouble he had been at in collecting them. In order to this, he set before him a sack of wheat, as it had just been threshed out of the sheaf. He then bid him pick out the chaff from among the corn, and lay it aside by itself. The Critic applied himself to the task with great industry and pleasure; and after having made a due separation, was presented by Apollo with the chaff for his pains* !"

---

* Spectator, Vol. IV. No. 291.

ADVERTISEMENT.

———

THE circumstances which form a principal feature in the following Tale, are said to have *actually* occurred, some time during the latter part of the last Century; and whatever may have been added in the colouring, the outline, doubtless, will readily be recognised. But, (let me observe here) though it hath now fallen to my lot to paint the *dark* side of the picture, it may yet be mine to display, in contrast, the all-radiant beam of that loveliness which *can* emanate alone from—WOMAN; *that* which is, which must be, the *natural* state even of her, who

" *For an apple damn'd mankind.*"

CONTENTS.

ERRATA.

COUNTERFEIT SAINTS, Canto II. Stanza 50, Line 2, *for* " fogot," *read* " forgot."
DR. MAC SAP, Page 98, Line 9, *for* " head," *read* " heed."
—— 103, —— 9, *for* " then," *read* " than."
OMAR, —— 144, —— 16, *for* " weigh'd by," *read* " weigh'd down by."

THE

Counterfeit Saints, &c.

———

CANTO I.

◆

◆

1.

In Popish times—but when, I can't determine,—
  Two noted rogues, who liv'd upon their wit,
(One I'll call Martin, and the other, Hermon,
  Because it suits me now to rhyme with it;
And since 'tis said, there's " magic in a name,"
This, for what I know, may have lawful claim!)

B

2.

Sneak'd to hear Mass, and with becoming gravity,

    Plac'd themselves coolly by a maiden old,

Who view'd the lads with tolerable suavity,

    Considering she was one of ancient mould.

One of the breed, we term, cross-grain'd and peevish,

Rich, and inimical to fingers *thievish !*

3.

Mayhap, you'll fancy that the rogues' transgressions

    Had brought them moping to the Virgin's shrine,

To tease her ladyship with large confessions,

    And keep the holy Fathers from their wine :

No, no—the virgin that they came to woo,

Was this old maiden that they stuck so to

4.

'Tis true, in general, rogues will seldom venture

    Into a Popish church to pop a snout,

For fire and brimstone, smelling as they enter,

    They're very glad indeed to pop it out;

And really, Purgatory's fire and smoke,

Whatever you may think it, is no joke !

5.

And then your Friars! oh! they're keen-eyed fellows,
  That to the pocket keep a wondrous look-out,
And never fail to blow the brimstone bellows,
  Till they contrive the glittering bits to book out;
Until, in short, you make *them* restitution,
The dogs will never give you absolution.

6.

'Tis said, that once a young repentant sinner
  Return'd the total profit of his trading,
And vow'd, that ere he went to eat his dinner,
  He'd give his freakish conscience an unlading;
So to a holy Friar straight he comes,
And thus exclaims, with sundry hás and hums!—

7.

" Father, I have been wicked, very wicked
  " I robb'd a lady of a splendid trinket;
" A Jew—(but hang it, that's no harm) I tricked   "
  " Indeed, my son, a heinous crime I think it;
" Give me the jewel."   Cried the youth, " Good lack!
" Justice impell'd me, and I took it back."

8.

" You took it back, you dog! oh, blessed Virgin,

    " Nathless the foul impurities you gave ;

" Prodigious guilt ! but mark me —from a scourging

    " Not e'en his Holiness of Rome can save !"

" But how then, Father—if I steal 't again ?"

" How then, you rogue ?—why *I'll* absolve you then !"

9.

But to my story, without further prosing :

    The rascal wights, who now at Mass appear'd,

Watching a lucky moment, when, half dozing,

    The pious maiden's chin had downward steer'd,

And (for in cone-like form this chin did fair look,)

Hid half its longitude beneath her pray'r-book.

10.

And where's the wonder if you catch her napping ?

    What can be done when *spirits* overpow'r us?

What tow'r can stand, when floods like these are sapping,

    And spite of heav'nly intercession bore us ?

Yes, though she pray'd as oft as priests could let her,

Spirits of evil ever got the better !

11.

This case was very grievous—trust my word—
　　Especially with all her predilection
For holy monks : 'tis true I never heard
　　That *nuns* had this same share in her affection ;
But that might possibly arise from this,
Her stars decreed her—an unmarried Miss.

12.

And I've observ'd sometimes your ancient ladies
　　Love e'en *automatons* in man's shape well—
Because it happens, having pass'd their hey-days,
　　They hate th' appendage—" leading apes in hell ;"
And then too, like *our* fair one, they confide,
Something too much, upon their *spiritual* guide.

13.

This caus'd, though it be strange, her non-devotion,
　　And bless'd the knaves with famous opportunity,
To prove to nicety, a pretty notion—
　　All means are just and fair in this community ;
Nay, if the fact's not monstrously belied,
'Tis so in more communities beside.

14.

But what communities? perhaps you ask;

   That's more than I have bargain'd to unfold:

And verily 't would be no easy task,

   To mention all the amorous of gold!

Go to commercial men ; I warrant there

You'll find enough to make the wisest stare!

15.

You'll find—but hush! 'tis dangerous to enter

   Too deep into the muddy waves of trade ;

Let me in time retreat, ere peradventure,

   The *grizzled owl* * with flapping wings invade ;

Th' attack were far too terrible to stand—

And shots like mine must penetrate from land!

---

* A species of *sea-bird*, which, though unnoticed by naturalists, may often be seen hovering about places of trade ; when perfectly tamed, they are found of great use to mercantile men, having (in common with *other* owls) the property of seeing distinctly in the *darkest* places, and are chiefly caught dabbling in the *dirtiest!*

16.

'Tis fit, that here I call to recollection,

 Your Popish folk of ev'ry sort and nation,

Believe most cordially, and hate reflection :

 Enough, and more, they think to gain salvation* !

Now, this most venerable Fair possess'd

Double the quantity of all the rest.

17.

Such, knew the rogues; intent, as I was saying,

 To seize a time the lady to cajole,

Who now slept soundly, when she should be praying

 And reck'ning beads to save her sinful soul,

Which, if she had been doing, 'stead of dreaming,

Unlucky had it been for all their scheming!

18.

Nor would th' excrescence, I denominated

 A tapering chin, have dropt in such degree,

---

* " Nobis profanis ista *(Evangelia)* legere non licet sed *sacer-dotibus* duntaxat!'" was the reply of a Catholic, on being recommended to peruse his Bible !

As to be seen (think not I over-rate it)

    Better than half a foot below the knee—

Which certainly must be, in ev'ry sense,

Confess'd a dreadful inconvenience.

19.

However, to assist the scheme projected,

    (And which to tell ye, I too long delay)

Such glorious chance was not to be neglected,

    And fate supply'd but little time to stay ;

For just as they had whipt beneath her snout

A letter, lo ! her eye-balls roll'd about !

20.

No—there I'm wrong ; they did not roll exactly.

    Because they long had pass'd their rolling days ;

So fix'd within their sallow lids compactly,

    And in oblique directions shot their rays ;

From either corner did the beams come glancing,

Like light in *ball-rooms* to assist your dancing.

21.

Thus wak'd the maid ; and in her cogitation,

    Wonder'd kind heav'n should impose sobriety :

But then, thought she, " I'm sure of *my* salvation,

 " Because I make it up by piety :

" Besides, all other virtues I'm not poor in—

" Bless'd Virgin! *did* they overhear me snoring ?"

22.

This thought, upon their pivots turn'd her goggles

 A modicum or so—just as you've seen

A little truant brat, alarm'd at boggles,

 In some lone place, where he should not have been ;

Or love-sick lad, expecting on the mow

His fair one—clasp (oh sad mischance !) the cow.

23.

But when imagining that all securely,

 Her soporiferous habits kept from view,

She turn'd her eye-lids down again demurely,

 As ev'ry pious maiden ought to do ;

When lo! with proper quantum of surprise,

A gay bespangled letter struck her eyes.

24.

Safely deliver'd of a wondrous cargo

 Of interjections, " bless més !" and all that,

B 5

Which on my credit, gentle reader, are no

    Small interlopers in a lady's chat ;

Like other dames, too curious long to linger,

She plac'd th' epistle 'twixt her thumb and finger.

25.

Oh! but it were a glorious sight to see

    The frowsy lass on this, now that side turn it.

Devoutly wond'ring, " what it ere could be,"

    And from the outside trying to discern it:

Then often. ere she ventur'd to unclose,

Cock and re-cock her specs upon her nose.

26.

Such ancient, handsome sort of spectacle,

    In modern days, undoubtedly you've seen,

If e'er by chance you sat in a conventicle,

    Drawn from an antique case of smart shagreen,

Whose rigid owners, as it well behoves 'em,

Fix on the nostril, when the Spirit moves 'em.

27.

If you *have* seen the spectacle I speak of,

    You then will have some notion too of Miss's,

And not of them alone, it may be, eke of
   Her thousand indescribables ; and this is
As much as I can say :—for want of better,
I'll on—and tell ye more about the letter.

28.

I think I said before, it was bespangled—
   With Loves and Graces (*French* ones, tho', I mean),
Also from either side of it there dangled
   A piece of ribbon of celestial sheen ;
(But by the way, my nag of thought miscarries,
Or I'd have said, long since, we were at Paris!)

29.

Julie (so call her) snapt the seal armorial ;
   And as the wax surrender'd up its trust,
There burst upon her aged eyes a glory all
   Unknown before to " *vessels form'd of dust** ;"
And thus, as nearly as I can define,
In lofty language, ran the strain divine :—

---

  * A phrase frequently used by the Hero of a Conventicle.
" Spargere qui somnos *cantu*que *manu*que solebat."—VIRGIL.

THE LETTER.

30.

The grateful odour of thy prayers, oh maiden,
   On Zephyr's wings to Heav'n hath been transported,
Which never yet were known as sweetly laden—
   At least I cannot find it so reported,
Wherefore belov'd! on this consideration,
I feel for thee a monstrous inclination.

31.

And know, by favour yet unprecedented,
   (Be joyful, Julie, cast away all sorrow)
I, even I, to quit will be contented,
   The bow'rs of bliss, and sup with thee to-morrow
But, pray, no ceremony—don't be queasy—
We holy Gentlemen are free and easy!

32.

But for this privilege the most uncommon,
   Remember I especially entreat,
E'en on your life, the wonder tell to no man,
   That I a mortal condescend to meet.
Bless, bless thy lot, so full of richest promise,
And wait the coming of thy friend
                 St. THOMAS.

33.

Reader! it is the case with ev'ry woman,
    At least, with all of whom I ever heard ;
No matter, if from Protestant or Roman,
    They still give credit to a sugar'd word !
Tell 'em they're beautiful, and they'll not let it
By you forgot be—or themselves forget it.

34.

Is it not true, fair Dames, what I have written?
    You, all of you, *are* beautiful, ne'er doubt it ;
For varying fancy with a charm is smitten,
    Only for something *Hottentot* about it !
Some like a six foot grace, whilst others gape
In admiration of an oval shape.

35.

Some doat on many a round-about of fat,
    Whilst *lean* ones, put each feature in distortion
And I must say there something is in *that,*
    For largest women bring the largest *portion !*
But hold—and let me not neglect Miss Julie,
Who read—and need I add—believ'd it duly !

36.

Such grace, she thought, was but the meet reward
  That all her piety deserv'd t' inherit;
And that's a point most ladies would think hard
  To be deny'd—I mean reward of merit!
And here her *faith* (great article of creed!)
Did her most wondrous services indeed.

37.

Yet if you but consider for a second,
  There's nothing very wonderful, that's certain,
Women and vanity are justly reckon'd
  So much allied, that age's thick-wrought curtain
Nor hides, nor lessens.   Who can then compute
Th' effect of these and bigotry to boot?

38.

Oh! they have faith to swallow mountains—carry
  Olympus balanc'd on a needle's point!
And nothing more absurd, that doctrine, marry!
  Than those the fabling Popish priests have coin'd;

Witness the bottle where the holy tears dropp'd*;
'Fore Jove! th' inventor well deserv'd his ears cropp'd!

39.

Yet I'm afraid, if all who deal in fiction,
   Were by the law compell'd to lose their ears —
I would not have ye think it sland'rous diction —
   But nine in ten would feel the want of theirs;
And then the fashion, 'mid newspaper cries,
Would be, "*false ears*," as well as teeth and eyes.

40.

As for the nymphs, oh! grief above all other,
   (If loss of *ears* produce a loss of *hearing*,)
For who sage curiosity could smother,
   As to forego a pleasure *so* endearing?
Why faith, the injury would be exceeding,
And put a total stop to *slander breeding*!

---

* Alluding to the tricks of the Roman Catholic Clergy.
" The church of the patron of Thessalonica (says Gibbon, inter
cætera) was served by the canons of the Holy Sepulchre, and
contained a divine o ntment, which distilled daily and stupendous
miracles!" And such *distilleries* are yet boasted of!

41.

I must confess, it doth surprise me much
   That 'mongst the taxes in the land appearing,
The ministers forget to have a touch
   At that prolific one—a tax on *hearing*;
And more especially, since well agreeing
With that *light* tax already upon *seeing*!

42.

If such should be the case, I'll make a bet,
   Within one twelvemonth from the present minute,
Ladies alone would pay the nation's debt;
   A serious subject—tho' there's nothing in it!
The nation is a debtor, let me say,
That pays all debts, but those it ought to pay.

43.

Now much and grievously did Julie fidget,
   More nervous far than e'en a modern fair,
Invoking saints, *viz.* Ursula or Bridget,
   Against th' expected moment to prepare:
Trembling, lest he should come in such great splendour,
That lightning flashing from his eyes should end her!

44.

" But, oh! what shall I give him," thought Miss Julie,

" Can holy spirits feed on mortal dishes?

" Perhaps ragoûts or patés, or more truly,

" Small limbs of chickens may provoke his wishes;

" Yet, as I am a sinner, I declare,

" I thought your saints had always liv'd on air!"

45.

In such dilemma, she resolv'd t' acquaint

Her maid Annette, with this proud visitation,

And ask if *she* knew how to feed a saint

With dishes wholly void of profanation.

Withal she bade her strictly, to discover

To none, the coming of this heav'nly lover.

46.

Unlike her mistress, was the fair Annette,

(Except, indeed, she was no wit, less simple)

Her cheek was beauty's heav'nliest amulet,

And love, arch-smiling, beam'd thro' ev'ry dimple;

Who saw, would fancy her a goddess; still he

Would find her *woman*—and but very silly!

47.

In consultation deep, the two long sat,
   Profoundly argumentative, be sure ;
But this, the sage result of all their chat
   To send for supper from a fam'd traiteur!
And so Annette was order'd to bespeak
Something at once *superbe et magnifique!*

48.

Nor ended here the lady's wondrous ardour,
   To greet the saint with quaint devices new ;
For as hope whisper'd he would well reward her,
   She deem'd it only what she ought to do!
So to a jeweller's (her kinsman he)
She sent for gems, and plate's rich marquetry '

49.

Who was there now like Julie so elate,
   Whilst at the toilette's pleasurable duty?
Her scraggy neck drawn up in lofty state,
   With best Parisian *rouge* improv'd her beauty ;
Stays grasp'd her angel form—her shoulders padded ;
Dales rose to hills—to plains were mountains added.

50.

Odours of all sorts, choicest aromatics,

   A perfect inundation did she pour;

And to a nose of quick perception, that speaks

   A wish to be far sweeter than before:

And truly, (tho' I won't defile my metre)

Vague rumour whispers that she *might* be sweeter!

51.

Now rigg'd in all her glory, Julie sat,

   Impatient, ay as boarding-school young misses,

Forc'd to endure a world of prudent chat,

   Tho' panting for a lover's ardent kisses;

Oblig'd to curb a potent inclination,

For such a trifle as—a reputation!

52.

Methinks I see, (behind a hawthorn cow'ring)

   The eager lover, often slyly peep

With staring eyes, and brow with anger low'ring,

   Cursing his evil stars, till half asleep;

Or else, perhaps, to while away the time,

" Stanzas to Night" assume the shape of rhyme!

53.

Julie, it really glads me to rehearse,

 Somehow had got a kind of knack at rhyming;

And tho' she car'd not sixpence for the verse,

 She ever felt delighted with the chiming;

These call'd she, " *Pearls of Poesy*," and strung 'em

Like holy beads—nay, to oblige ye, sung 'em!

54.

In days of old, as facts before us teach,

 Nymphs could make pretty verses, when at dusk a

" *Mournful murmur stray'd**," and doubtless, each

 Anna Matilda charm'd a Della Crusca!

Good heav'n! how sweet, to bosoms sympathetic,

To mourn in rhyme—fall sick, without emetic!

---

* See the sympathetic effusions of two sensitive souls, whose inflammability was such, that the very coruscations which *threatened* to dazzle the world, through the medium of a daily print, communicated the soft sigh of despondency and love, from the " *amiable*" youth to the " *bewitching*" fair one!

55.

Nay, some young ladies can, the Lord be thanked,

　　In verse be *mute*, as any pickled herring,

When wrapt in flannel petticoat or blanket,

　　The spirit or the muse within is stirring!

I've heard of nymphs who (but *that* plot miscarried)

Wrote, till they fancied they were really married!

56.

'Tis strange, how fast this fancy oft will hurry on;

　　Rarely indeed is found the least impediment,

That does not serve more speedily to spur ye on,

　　Altho' the top be scum, the bottom sediment;

'Tis a gay frostwork, (and tho' little matter it)

Next morn repairs, e'en if the tempest shatter it!

57.

Deeming Annette a long, a tedious while,

　　With high-rais'd expectations floating round—

Julie at loss the moments to beguile,

　　Thus gently twitter'd concords of sweet sound,

(Altho' her maid declar'd -- but who'll believe her?

Far sweeter sounds the marrow-bone and cleaver!)

JULIE'S SONG.

TO A TANSY.

1.

THEE, sweet Flow'r,
    When a-budding,
Men dèvour
    In a pudding.

2.

St. Bridget, bad men
    Only do it;
Time shall come, when
    They will rue it!

---

* To imagine a reason for Julie's selection of a "Tansy," to string her "pearls" upon, were no easy task; but we *may* still have recourse to that infallibly convincing argument every woman so well understands, viz. "*because she did.*"

3.

Only think, now,

(Oh the wretches!)

Not to let grow

Loveliest vetches.

4.

Ah! 'twill break my

Heart, or near it;—

I know not why,

Yet I fear it.

5.

Mercy sweet is,

Bright and charming,

And most meet is

For the *carmen**.

---

* Let not the fair admirer of " *pearls*," be deceived by the cacophany of this unhappy word. Think not the heroine of *our* verse would condescend to hold communication with *carmen!*— No, no—in the mysteries of her *latinity*, she was ever esteemed

6.

Bless my (heav'n's race !)

   Muse and metre ;

Then reviews base

   Daren't ill treat her.

7.

Then shall glory

   Deck my strains, and

My proud story

   Evermore stand !

58.

Whilst Julie, thro' her last remaining pegs,

   (Which you may fancy *wise* ones, if you will)

Thus trill'd forth her best tones, so sweet, efegs !

   " The air, a charter'd libertine, was still* !' "

---

more profoundly scientific, than can be conceived by the super-
ficial capacities of modern days! Besides, it is said,

      ——" Minuentur atræ

  Carmine curæ."—Hor.

      ——" That when he speaks,

The air, a charter'd libertine, is still."—SHAK. HEN. V.

But whether charm'd by harmony or no,
Alack, is more than I have pow'r to show !

59.

It's more than I have pow'r to show—because
   I was not there—nor can I ascertain it;
And, therefore, by indisputable laws*,
   'Tis clear, I cannot possibly explain it;
But notwithstanding this, I trust you pant to
Pass on with me into the Second Canto!

---

* Vide " Locke on the *Understanding.*"

END OF CANTO FIRST.

CANTO II.

―――

"' And now St. Peter at Heav'n's wicket, seems
To wait them with his keys."—MILTON.

―――

1.

Tʜᴀᴛ " Patience is a Virtue," all agree,
   And laud it too ; yet still on most occasions,
(And so, at least, the thing appears to me)
   Folks wish to make—a virtue of Impatience :
That Julie thus the maxim verified,
Must not, because it cannot, be denied !

2.

Oh ! she was full of *very* pious fears,
   Lest the great saint at last refuse to meet her ;
At ev'ry rap, the clouded feature clears—
   Yet enter not—no, not one saint-like creature ;

c 2

And then, (as oft you see for loss at Ombre)
The lady's face assum'd a tinge quite sombre.

3.

I would not have you think that Miss was amorous,
   Tho' it doth seem particularly funny—
Not, perhaps, that she felt a little clamorous,
   But that she parted freely with her money;
That circumstance, indeed, there's no disguising,
And still it's no less true, than it's surprising!

4.

My muse would joyfully explain th' event;
   Yet, as she cannot, (and it grieves me too)
I'll term it, at hap-hazard, " cent. per cent.,"
   And leave the problem to be solv'd by you:
Not that I really think she meant to play so;
Indeed I should be quite asham'd to say so!

5.

But still, if things *did* take a turn *outré*,
   She could not well reject them, to be sure,
For tho' her modesty might answer, " nay,"
   Will—would vociferate, " *de tout son cœur!*"

And horrid 'twere to give a saint refusal,
Whose voice mellifluous beats the lark or ousel!

6.

But to Annette, 'tis fit I turn my tale,
   (The maid of burning eye and rosy cheek)
And hoist before the breeze my scudding sail,
   To the far haven I have yet to seek ;
But ye, whose livers overflow with bile,
At least be *silent,* if ye cannot smile.

7.

First *au restaurateur,* in haste she posted,
   To order this grand supper—nor in vain ;
Annette, indeed, most confidently boasted,
   It beat all ever heard of in Cocaigne* ;
" Oh ! it is," oft in great delight, she cried,
" Sweetest of all the world can shew beside!"

---

* " Pais, où le ciel offie les viandes toutes cuites, et où comme on paile, les alouettes tombent toutes roties."—DUCHAT.

8.

But you may well believe, no small surprise

   In the restaurateur was thus excited;

He twirl'd aloft the whites of both his eyes,

   With an arch leer, that spoke him much delighted;

" I know Madame *can* pay," he said internally,

" And she *shall* pay, and that too most infernally.

9.

" And yet 'tis very strange," continued he,

   " What can the old lass want with such a supper?

" She's superannuated, and may be

   " Has taken *by mistake* an extra cup; or,

" Probably, she's mad; however, I know

" All *my* concern is, to procure the rhino."

10.

Away from this most *conscientious* Dripping,

   (In England, verily, they're much the same)

Behold the fair Annette so gaily tripping

   On to the jeweller's—Guillaume, his name;

And after sundry turns about and bending,

She reach'd the threshold, whither she was wending

11.

Seest thou the maiden's cheek, with crimson flushing
    Sudden, as caus'd by some all-pow'rful spell?
In former days, this was consider'd *blushing*,
    But what you term it now, I cannot tell;
For truly, (ladies don't be in a passion)
Blushing has long been wholly out of fashion!

12.

But Annette blush'd—ay deeply blush'd, young ladies,
    And can ye not the wondrous cause discover?,
I guess a few of ye'd increase your *pray-days*
    For such a reason—'twas, ye gods—a lover!
But then he was (doubtless, great discontent is)
Only a goldsmith's journeyman-apprentice.

13.

Yet, still he *was* a lover, spruce and comely,
    And to Annette it was sufficient quite.
I am not certain, were he poor and homely,
    Whether so *much* she would have lov'd the wight.
Homely and rich has quite another sound;
And as to worth, you weigh that by the *pound*.

14.

Ambrose *had* wealth, and she would fain possess it ;

    Therefore, no doubt, the couple meant to marry,

Unless (I don't affirm, altho' I guess it)

    A larger fish the bait away should carry ;

For tho' I term'd her *silly*, (Fame doth bark it)

She ever kept an eye upon the *market!*

15.

Ambrose, it seems, was now the best that offer'd,

    And so, for him, her ruby lips shed kisses ;

And by fair Venus, they were nought to scoff at ;

    Few others yielded half so many blisses !

Blisses, in truth, that bade that happy swain

Who once had sipt, oft haste to sip again !

16.

Oh! I remember One, whose lips a fountain

    Of nectar'd kisses seem'd—full, rich, and dewy ;

Hang it! I almost fancied I could count 'em,

    Fix'd on their rosy beds.   Altho', 'tis true, I

Have gaz'd at beauty, hours of life's short span,

Yet, the like saw I never—never can.

17.

But 'twas not lips alone, nor sparkling eyes,—

   Sweetest expression o'er each feature rov'd ;

I do not think there lives a man so wise,

   That could behold such excellence unmov'd ;

And yet, (deuce take the women, I say) yet

This perfect beauty was a sad coquette* !

18.

I fear me too, Miss Julie's pretty wench,

   The fair Annette, had notions of coquetting ;

Indeed, it is a thing so truly French,

   The word is but a stone in English setting ·

So long we've had it too, you well may doubt

If Nature meant the land to be without.

19.

But we *have* got it, and I'm sorry for't,

   'Tis such a paltry piece of affectation,

---

* Should this *faint* portrait ever meet the eye of her for whom
it was drawn, and *that* eye acknowledge its resemblance, let her
be thankful for the hint, and appear what nature first intended—
" wisest, virtuousest, discreetest, best !"

Brought o'er by some lost character at Court,
  Who'd no necessity for reputation.
Fashion spreads fast, from shore to shore we find,
As chaff is toss'd on all sides by the wind!

20.

The vermeil blush, by this, had slipt her cheek of.
  Yet her bright eyes she still did sweetly cover;
For oh! how was it possible to speak of
  One earthly thing, whilst looking at a lover ?
Her little heart, in truth, was very *tumorous;*
And as for glances, why they were innumerous'

21·

Ambrose, delighted, roll'd his roguish eye,
  And verily seem'd ready to devour her;
And let me just inform you, by the bye,
  That *was* almost enough to overpow'r her'
But tho' she didn't faint, *la delicatesse*
Made her extremely nervous, ne'ertheless.

22.

After some pretty hesitations ended,
  He ventur'd to inquire her pleasure there;

And with the finest of confusions blended,

   She summon'd resolution to declare:

And most magnanimous it was, no doubt

What! have a secret, and not let it out!

23.

That it was difficult, I need not paint;

   And she'd have told it, but the anger dreaded,

Not of Madame alone, but of the Saint,

   To whom she judg'd her mistress would be wedded;

And, therefore, told him merely of their want

Of some rich gems and plate—*tres elegantes.*

24.

Had Jove " *omnipotens,*" (with all the thunder

   They flog perforce, at school, into one's pate)

Come rattling past him—not with half the wonder,

   Had he been rous'd—as now, to hear her state

Miss Julie's wants.   Not stranger was it, when

Circe transform'd a herd of hogs to men*!

---

  * A race, whose *hoggish* propensities have, I believe, since then
but little varied.   We have still, thank Heaven! *princes* and no-
bles of the " *true legitimate cut!*"

25.

" O mon Dieu," exclaim'd the astonish'd lad,

 " Is Madame, (thus by courtesy they call her)

" Is Madame Julie then, become quite mad?

 " The saints forbid such misery befall her !

" Diable! what wants she with plate or jewel?

 " Make her, Annette, a plate of *water gruel!*"

26.

" Pray, don't be quite so saucy, Mr. Ambrose,"

 Replied the fair, with anger-lighted eyes

And smiling scorn, turn'd up her lovely nose,

 " Really one might suppose you wondrous wise;—

" But, Sir, we want, and we *will* have the plate too,

" You ugly wretch,—how *heartily* I hate you !"

27.

Nay, nay now, dearest, sweetest, best Annette,

 " Can you inflict a punishment so cruel?

" I meant not, love, to put you in a pet,

 " Altho' I mentioned water—*water-gruel.*"

This was a specimen of joke, you see,

For gruel nourish'd Julie's piety.

28.

Howe'er, submission and a dose of flattery,

　　Clos'd up the breach that anger made before,

As light (a poet tells us, is term'd " _scattery*_ ")

　　Bedawbs the world, and darkness is no more ;

Indeed it must be false, what libels teach us,

Women are ever found good-natur'd creatures !

29.

And soon Annette smooth'd her contracted brows,

　　While sweetest smiles, like fairy visions spring,

That, mocking all the ecstacies they rouse,

　　Elude the grasp, yet chide the lingering !

And Ambrose, all but hope's gay dreams forgetting,

Smil'd at the maiden's pleasure in coquetting.

---

* Vide a " Story of Rimini," by L—— H——

　　" Who had stout notions on the _scribbling_ score."

　　　　　　　　　　　　　　　　　　　　　　Idem.

　　　" It was a pity—so it was,

　" That villainous _affectation_ should be digg'd

　" Out of the bowels" of so _fair_ a soil.

　　　　　　　　Hotspur's Description of a Coxcomb.

30.

But Ambrose was a cunning dog; he spy'd
    Some mystery with her request connected;
Miss Julie never had before applied
    For plate—nor was it now to be expected;
Hers was no house of gaiety; and, therefore,
'Twas doubly wonderful what these things were for '

31.

Touch but the *secret spring*, and all can tell,
    (At least all those who pore upon *romances*)
The pannel flies—and deeds that darken hell*,
    Or, bags of shiners†, meet your searching glances!
And Ambrose tried the ways maids deem enchanting,
To gain th' intelligence that he was wanting.

32.

The girl had made her mind up, to declare
    The wondrous secret, long before she told it;

---

   * As in the " Old English Baron."
   † As in the " Mysteries of Udolpho," and other *mysteries*—
passim.

But then he coax'd her so charmingly—did swear
    Such pretty oaths of love; that still to hold it
Her panting bosom strove: *there* secrets lie,
    Like full-fledg'd birds—the first fair day, they fly !

33.

Think ye that birds their young ones can retain,
    Longer than they have means and place to soar ?
Not they; and secrets in love's nest remain,
    You may believe it, not a minute more :
I'd trust a secret with a lady too —
But one I car'd not if the kingdom knew.

34.

Annette, indeed, made many a long demur,
    As if, to tell, or not to tell, contesting ;
But that was *sauce piquante* to give a spur,
    And make the story doubly interesting :
At length it came, and he was bade, " *discover*
" *To none, the coming of this heav'nly lover !*"

35.

If Ambrose was surprised before, I'm curst,
    If now he was not petrified with wonder ;

He stood—not as my simile describ'd the first—

    But just as if he'd *gorg'd* a bolt of thunder,

Which Jove dispatch'd from his celestial store,

    Pop thro' his jaws, and screw'd him to the floor !

36.

But when, at last, his tongue had found a voice,

    'Twas not a *member* ever fond of speaking,

Whence all the house re-echoes to its noise—

    But rather like a water-barrel leaking ·

A gentle voice it was, whose tame condition

Knew no alternative, than *meek submission** !

---

  * Sir William C—t-s's " meek submission" to his " *noble friend*," excellently illustrates the text ! 'Tis a singular coincidence, that Horace in the Ninth Satire of the First Book, should (as if anticipating Sir William's political feelings) exclaim in astonishment,

    ————————" vin tu,

    Curtis, Judæis * oppedere?"

No one, however, can for a moment imagine, the Baronet's rotundity, or his *eloquent* speeches, bear any resemblance to a " *water-barrel leaking.*"

    * Judæis—*well* translated " Ministers."

37.

Such *may* be found; and wary Ambrose dreaded
    Again to see his mistress in a fury.
" Only," thought he, " let's wait till we are wedded,
    " And then I'll show who's master, I assure you;
" But Madame wed a saint! Lord, what a joke—
" Straw blazes high, but finishes in smoke '"

38.

It cannot be suppos'd that perfect credit
    By Ambrose should be given to the tale ;
But tho' he deem'd it false, think not he said it,
    For well he knew how little 't would avail.
Full steadily doth superstition run
Darkling along, despite the beaming sun!

39.

The goldsmith was from home; this Ambrose stated;
    And so the maid, alack! must wait content!
But he resolv'd the tale should be related,
    Before or plate or gems to Julie went;
Yet, that the time might swiftly glide along,
Annette agreed to charm him with a song.

40.

Of *course*, it was not without much entreaty ;

But that you readily may understand ;

Because young Misses think it very pretty,

Never to sing, or *squall*, at first command :

Yet did *she* sing, (and when does flattery fail?)

As to the rose, th' enamour'd nightingale* !

ANNETTE'S SONG.

1.

WHERE yon elm trees that loftily wave in the wind,

Afford a cool shade from the sun's dreaded heat,

On a couch overspread with sweet flow'rs I reclin'd,

And my heart in my bosom tumultuously beat ;

I ponder'd—and what was it on, do you think?

Why, on Love; for last night I could scarce sleep a wink.

---

* Such an opportunity to introduce this *lady-like* simile was not to be lost sight of. The nightingale (and the " τὸ ῥόδον τῶν ἐρώτων,") is become so exclusively the property of the fair sex, that their throats might not, I think, be inaptly termed, " *Nightingale Lane.*"

2.

So this morning I rose, (as I usually do,
    When tir'd of lying,) and hither I came;
And I trust you will think it was wonderful too—
    My heart, like the sun, appear'd all in a flame!
And I felt—(oh! for me may some kind breast be
      yearning)
I felt with delightfullest love I was burning.

3.

But, still as I ponder'd, big sighs that were hatching
    Fann'd the flame, till it blaz'd at a terrible rate,
And I found that the parts all adjacent were catching;
    'Tis true, on my word, tho' I'm sorry to say't;
Then I said, " Ah! if such be the state of the weather,
" Heart, body and all, will be burnt up together!"

4.

Now I turn'd my eyes downward; but sorrow still
    springs—
    Dandelions* and daisies, all seem'd to complain;

---

* I ought here to take occasion to say something *smart* against
that unfortunate race of beings, " the Dandies:" but I pass

For they hung down their heads, *pretty innocent things*ᶻ .

Tho' I fervently hope they'll be happy again!

Alas! I had press'd there—oh! do not condemn—

I painfully feel—*much* too heavy for them!

5.

Why, *why* did I ramble, recline 'neath the trees,

And cruelly injure what Nature has sown?

Forgive, oh! forgive, and in future, the ease

Of sweet flow'rs I'll consult, ere I think of my own;

And *if* I survive, a fine sonnet I'll pen;

But never, oh never, be wicked again!

———

(however reluctantly) the opportunity, and only request the gen-
tle reader to turn his eye to the first newspaper within reach—
there he will find much of what was doubtless *intended* to be good
—and the intent alone *is* " good in law!"

　　* I have indisputable authority for the epithets here applied;
viz. that of Mr. Wordsworth, " The orb of whose genius (as he
himself *candidly* enough confesses) is gloriously resplendent."
Vide Wordsworth's Poems.

41.

What is it man's dull way thro' life beguiles,

    And brightens up his day?   'Tis love, 'tis love!

Like the fair insect which at midnight smiles,

    And gaily sparkles in the desert grove.

What is it helps to eke out many a sonnet?

'Tis love, 'tis love—you may depend upon it'

42.

Since such, then, are the proud excess of glories

    That circle love, why faith it isn't queer.

(For women ever are invet'rate Tories

    In love affairs!) the maid should sing on't here;

Altho', perhaps, (yet grieving is but folly!)

The mournful strain may make ye melancholy.

43.

Ambrose—it almost is beyond belief—

    Was so affected, salt tears ran each cheek off;

But if they ran from *laughter* or from *grief*,

    The chronicle I quote, forgets to speak of;

So curiosity I cannot sate—or

Could I—what would be left my *commentator* ?

44.

The song—which probably, the youth *encor'd,*

    Beguil'd the time, till Guillaume interrupted

The soothing cadence—and sweet peace restor'd,

    Whose virgin purity they had corrupted ;

Then Ambrose told his tale, but bade, " *discover*

" *To none, the coming of this heav'nly lover !*"

45.

Upon " *surprise,*" have I said much ; the rout it

    Doubtless hath made among the learned, may

Save me, the pain of lab'ring more about it,

    And leave me, freely to pursue my way !—

Suffice it then, our Goldsmith was astounded,

And worse than all—*confoundedly confounded** !"

46.

On some expedient to hit revolv'd he,

    With hasty step, parading to and fro,—

---

* Upon the excellence of this epithet, consult " Epithetonia !"
I flatter myself it is no way inferior to " *Confusion worse con-*
founded."—MILTON.

And after much deep thinking, thus resolv'd he:
　To do directly—what? He did not know!
He struck his forehead, it was hard and thick,
And might have been a tenement of brick.

47.

It sometimes happens, in the densest head,
　A bright thought rises—like rare birds that soar,
And by strange chance, to unknown lands are led
　A wondrous thing—none ever saw before!
So 'twas with Guillaume—like a flame it shone—
An ignis fatuus, scarcely seen, ere gone.

48.

But thus he did determine, all she wanted,
　Of plate and gems he'd send.　Then to complete her,
With glory yet unparalleled, he panted,
　To act himself heav'n's porter,—holy Peter;
Array'd in which disguise, he meant to wait,
Catch his gull'd saintship, and secure the plate!

49.

So off he sent Annette, to Julie,—whom
　We left poor creature, big with vast impatience

Her pious brow, had gain'd a holy gloom—

    Which it had known before, on some occasions

Occasions which—(God help a maiden Miss!)

Requir'd not half the temper, that did this.

50.

But now, the rascals—Martin and that Hermon,

    I told you of, (I hope you've not fogot 'em) ;

Who meant to read Miss Julie, such a sermon,

    As she'd remember long enough,—od rot 'em!

When ev'ning's shades slipt down, the former stole,

Unknown, unquestion'd to the splendid goal.

51.

But the last rogue,—videlicet—young Hermon,

    Station'd himself, as sentry at the door ;

The *very* spot, I'd willingly determine ;

    Only remember, what I said before :—

It would *so* vex the learned, when around 'em—

Lay piles of books, and nothing to confound 'em.

52.

When holy Thomas enter'd the saloon,

    By art adorn'd, as gaily as it could be,

Poor Julie, felt inclin'd to try a swoon,

    Only—she fear'd it indecorous would be;

Besides the saint—(a thing, alas how madding!)

Might then discover all the art of padding!

53.

Such thought, as I have heard, from heads profound,

    Hath *often* sav'd a lady from a fainting,

Lest it appear the form so plump and round,

    Turn *bolster'd*, and the lovely face—a painting* ;

But these *must* be aspersions,—all mere lies,

Nor if I *saw*, would I believe my eyes!

---

* " Ladies, conscious of no personal defects, and convinced
" of their *own* graces, may, upon occasion, drop into a faint;
" but I would earnestly caution them, first to provide *arms* and
" *supporters*—without which, this *carriage* of the fair one will only
" prove useless and empty show."—*Extract from an ancient Latin
Manuscript, now in the possession of the " Fudge Family."*

As to the *antiquity* of the faint, it cannot indeed be doubted;
Virgil himself says, " procumbit humi *bos*,"—the *lady* fainted!

54.

But who can wonder, at a lady's qualms,

    When a great Saint, thus popt himself before her—

Instant, she rais'd aloft, her wither'd palms;

    And humbly knelt his most profound adorer;

Yet ere we travel further, on our way,

How he was drest, 'twere not amiss to say.

55.

His garb was of the Jewish Patriarch kind—

    While from his chin, a reverend beard down flowing,

Prov'd— as it must, to ev'ry thinking mind;

    The monstrous length of time it had been growing,

But *where* it grew, in heav'n, or earth, or hell;

Ask the first *goat* you see—and it may tell!

56.

An antique book in very sumptuous gilding,

    From one arm apostollically fell,—

The other, a stout oaken sapling wielding,

    Seem'd to support his steps, extremely well;

Us'd as a horse, it may be, when the cloud

Opens its womb, and thunders roar aloud,

57.

For *such* were dang'rous riding! Julie's knees

   Bent in obsequious reverence to the rogue,

Who rais'd her up, politely as ye please,

   But told her praying—now was out of vogue* ;

And tho' he'd no *objection* to her mumming,

He trusted supper would be quick in coming!

58.

The lady, seem'd aghast, says our recorder,

   To hear this holy one, so strangely speak ;

However, keeping under, her disorder,—

   Thus she replied in lowly tones and meek.

" Oh ! thou all glorious, suffer me to thank,

" Your saintship for my elevated rank !"

59.

Here, let the muse, delay her wantonning,

   And as the heart, swells o'er the fated past,

---

* Are not the *" polite"* audience at St. James' pretty much of the same opinion? and may we not say with Horace, to most of such *congresses,* " Non es quod simulas."

Strike to deep notes of sorrow, the wild string—

    And (as she may), sweet mournful music cast;

For superstition comes, and woe the while,

Death sits exulting there, and courts her ghastly smile.

60.

And say—has blood yet ceased for her to flow,

    Does peace, to bless a wasted world appear?

Oh! do we not, too well—too dearly know,

    Her hated influence draws the bitter tear* ?

---

    * Spain, and her re-established Inquisition, need but be mentioned to demonstrate the truth of this position; but without wandering thither, let our domestic hearths, haunted as they too often are by this horrible demon, afford their lamentable proofs. The following account, extracted from undoubted sources, is of itself too dreadful to require additional comment, and may perhaps serve as a beacon to warn the slaves of superstition against the encroaches of their tyrannical oppressor!

    July, 1818.—" A few weeks back, a shocking murder was perpetrated at the village of Ower, near Galway, Ireland, on a woman named Flaherty. The husband of this woman, with her whole family, consisting of her father, mother, and two brothers, were led to imagine, that the deceased was possessed of some

Then be their none, that view our tale with scorn,

Eve, may have dangers—fatal as the morn !

61.

The rogue perceiving the last words he'd spoken,

   Had rous'd no little wonder in madame,—

Resum'd awhile, the silence he had broken,

   For his pulse beat, betokening some alarm ;

But soon, with solemn phiz, most energetically,

He spoke, altho' perhaps. too *hypothetically!*

62.

" Fair Julie,—the delight, the joy of heav'n,

   " Thy piety proclaims thee pious —very ;

" Ask therefore what thou wilt, it shall be giv'n,

   " And thou and I, to-night will be *right* merry ;

" But see—the supper waits us ! come my fair,

" Proud is Saint Thomas to conduct thee there."

---

evil spirit, and that the husband had power from the priest to effect a cure. Under this impression, her own family were not only induced to look on, but even to assist, while he strangled her, by putting a pair of iron tongs around her neck, and pressing them, till she expired. The father of this unhappy victim of superstition has been committed to the county gaol."

63.

Bounce, on her marrow-bones, once more fell Julie,

　　Remembering nought of what had pass'd before ;

And on this second fall, grown wiser truly ;

　　Martin spoke not, lest he should blunder more :

So having raised her, from her knees again—

She happy damsel was—he happy swain !

64.

Sage gluttons ! tho' at supper, if you look

　　For a description, you're mistaken much,

Because, I don't pretend to be a cook,

　　Tho' possibly indeed, you may be such ;

But still—(to make a final peroration),

I shall omit the *tempting* avocation* '

---

　　* " *Tempting*," in truth, if we may give credit to the cormorant appetite of your modern Epicure ! Astonishing as the assertion may appear, I was once gravely informed by one of the *genus*, that he supposed the chief part of happiness hereafter would be in *re-gorging* (so I understood him) the " *tid-bits*" which had so delectably tickled the palate upon earth ! !

65.

'Martin, might well be anxious to set to:

  Each *friandise*, he made so quickly fly,

That Julie, found she had enough to do,

  To follow all his motions with her eye!

At last, she deem'd it certain, that her guest,

Eat part, and sent to paradise the rest.

66.

But whilst she watch'd this *gourmand*, lo! a rapping—

  Like volleying thunder, o'er the cloud-capt hill:

Rous'd up Annette, who, wearied out, was napping

  To the deep base, her *minstrel* nose, did trill:

But soon its music hush'd, and nought around

Was heard, save that loud terrifying sound.

67.

The saint!—oh where was now, the holy saint!

  What was he doing, in this dreadful hour?

Alack? 'tis truth, and truth alone, I paint—

  He had no will to help, or will, no pow'r!

Louder, and louder, grew the outrageous knocking;

But Thomas bade her—" hold, forbear unlocking."

68.

Poor Thomas!—that celestial voracity

    Had stuck a something bony, in his Jaws,

And when the maid, with wondrous pertinacity

    Would ope the door, against his holy laws,

To bar th' endeavour, putting forth his strength,

The bony substance loos'd,—and tumbling came *at*

    length!

69.

But with great force it flew, and hit the girl,

    Who frighten'd beyond language to discover;

Believ'd the saint with dread, vindictive hurl,

    Had spit a thunder bolt—and all was over;

With a wild shriek, whose terrors can't be painted,

Turn'd pale as parsneps, and directly fainted.

70.

Guess, if you can, the mighty consternation,

    That siez'd Miss Julie, on her maiden's fall;

Her joy had risen, like an exhalation,

    And vanish'd just as speedily an' all;

She look'd at him imploringly and just,

Had bent in adoration to the dust.

71.

When that same door, they had so long been battering
    With a tremendous crash, gave way—and straight
In *twice three angels** rush, their hobnails clattering,
    Upon the pavement at a desp'rate rate;
But oh! 'tis most distressing to the muse,
These heav'nly spirits came in dirty shoes!

72.

Julie's grand staircase, was " *besmirch'd†*," in truth;
    But let not this afflict ye much, I pray,
Nor think celestials had so little ruth;
    These were but *angels*—" for the working day†."
In fact, they were—(nor better much than geese!)
A small detachment of the French police.

73.

Before them march'd along, most magisterially
    Enveloped in a Jewish gaberdine—

---

* " Sunt mihi *bis septem*," &c. &c.—VIRGIL.
† Shakspeare.

With a bald pate, that look'd—oh so imperially*,

    And reverend beard of most antique design ;

The great Saint Peter ! at whose side hung keys,

That lock and unlock heav'n's bright gates with ease.

74.

Fathers of learning, deeply read in Greek,

    Think—(and there seems much wisdom in the thought)

What we call *thunder*, only is the *creak*

    Of jarring gates, which Peter—as you're taught ;

Opes to let pass, with many bows and scrapes,

To vast varieties of lovely shapes !

75.

The truth of such a doctrine, I don't vouch,

    And all I've got to say of master Peter,

Is a warm hope, he bears not such a *pouch*

    As doth Saint Thomas,---such a monstrous eater ;

Or shrewdly I suspect, each *victualling* cargo,

That enter'd heav'n would suffer an embargo !

---

   * Hence, then, we observe, that the Emperor of Russia's *head
dress* is a palpable plagiarism !

76.

Julie, recover'd from each doubt and fear,

　When she beheld another saint's sweet face;

This night, she thought, would certainly appear,

　The whole, all-glorious apostolic race!

But mark, oh! mark, how fleetly joys fly from us,

As thus St. Peter did address St. Thomas.

77.

" Oh! Thomas, Thomas! how dar'st thou transgress

　" The laws that were to thee enjoin'd in beav'n?

" For set aside th' immoderate distress,

　" That must be mine forsooth; behold th' eleven

" With paradise lament, and all that be,

" Have left off singing to look after thee!

78.

" Now gentle Thomas,—pr'ythee onward troop;

　" Brief are the moments, giv'n thee too delay;

" Borne thro' dense clouds, by yon angelic group,

　" Thou'lt bend submissive, where I lead the way ·

" But as for you, madame, I do entreat,

" Have nought to do with *spirits* that can *eat*."

79.

Now whilst St. Peter, is haranguing, I

    May just return to Hermon, in the street,

Who could not fail, you may suppose, to spy

    This host of angels: when he saw them beat

Miss Julie's door, with such excessive clatter,

The rascal soon imagin'd, what was matter.

80.

Whisk! with a bullet's speed, he flies away,

    Onward and onward, not a jot delaying;

To an old chapel, where folks us'd to pray;

    Yet now, alas! but little us'd for praying!

It stood, " a ruin amid ruins,"—'round

Was nought but waste and desolation found.

81.

Here, in a subterranean recess,

    Dwelt imps of darkness—evil-doing dogs;

That like your lawyers, " *levy by distress**,*"

    And whom *too*, conscience very rarely jogs;

---

* " Thou wouldst know, if property be so safely guarded as
is generally believed. It is certain, that the whole power of a

Here they carouse, in diabolic glory,

And toast the rascals most renown'd in story.

82.

Hermon soon reach'd this place, such speed he made,

   And popping thro' the burrow, like a rabbit,

Quickly rous'd up his brethren in the trade,

   And bade *twice six* assume an angel's habit ;—

Disguises of all sorts, such lads provide,

Which hide their tricks,—when rogues have tricks to

     hide*

83.

The youth, himself became a second Peter,

   And with his troop, sped swiftly to the house ;

No wind, indeed, could possibly be fleeter,

   E'en tho' old Æolus the blast arouse !

---

king of England cannot force an acre of land from the weakest of his subjects ; but a *knavish attorney* will take away his whole estate by those very *laws* which were designed for its security."— *Persian Letters.*

       * Vide Pope's " Rape of the Lock."

   " Might hide her faults, if belles had faults to hide."

And Just as Peter Senior, with his crew,
Brought Thomas forth, the junior came in view.

84.

A dozen strapping fellows, against six,
    E'en magnanimity, I think must say,
(However we may " kick against the pricks,")
    Would hardly be in Britain thought fair play;
And Frenchmen, in such cases, are not nice,
Running, besides, is *national* exercise!

85.

So off ran Guillaume with the rest, and left
    Thomas to joy in this successful plan;
But ah! of what a strain, are you bereft—
    The fight of angels—and the full of man!
Oh! what great things, which *might* have come to light,
Are now enveloped in eternal night!

86.

Ay—fate is most omnipotent; and so
    I yield to fate.   Gladly would I rehearse
Some bloody desp'rate deed; because I know
    'Twould spin another canto into verse!

And yet, it may not be ; well! " *let that pass*,"
What is to be, *will* be ; what was to be so—*was!**

87.

St. Peter and St. Thomas now in union
 Enter'd again Miss Julie's ; and expounded
In earthly phrase,—how they in sweet communion
 Th' ambitious enemies of heav'n confounded ;
And then they said, a demon, most uncivil,
Had borrow'd Peter's form—to wit—the devil !

88.

That Uriel, an angel, quite respectable,
 Who lodges " *at the sun*,"—had seen him winging
To earth, and as it was from thence collectible
 To be no legal flight, directly ringing,
He sent a waiter with the strictest orders,
To watch the rebel spirit to earth's borders.

---

* I am told, this stanza is a *Byronism ;* I hope not—for,
  " Byron, with all thy faults, I love thee still!' "
But I fear this acknowledgment too much resembles the *gnat* upon
the *bull's horn !*

89.

There he beheld him take St. Peter's form,

   And then proceeding, the best road to Paris—

The waiter presently perceiv'd a storm;

   And so the news to Paradise he carries;

For Uriel's lodgings were remoter far,

Whilst Paradise was but a neighbouring star.

90.

" And Julie,"—thus went on the rogue St. Peter,

   " I wist St. Thomas had descended here,

" And Satan—who in truth's a clever cheater,

   " I judg'd might probably presume t'appear

" In arms, 'gainst him unarm'd and without aid,

" Which brought me too, oh! most immaculate maid.

91.

" But now sweet Saint! thy mission quick dispatch,

   " Time hurries onward at a fearful rate,

" And I the gates of Paradise must watch!"

   Said Thomas; " Julie, we do want thy plate,

" For a great feast is coming on, and we

" Do take it, for we love thy *piety!*"

92.

Are there who laugh at Julie's superstition,

   Wisely incredulous? Let such that are,

Turn their sagacious eyes; the same condition

   They'll find, I warrant, without glancing far!

Who tremble at the rustling leaf—nay boast,

To've seen the saucer eyeballs of a ghost?

93.

Who shudder, if perchance the salt be spilt?

   Who, if the knife and fork alack! be cross'd,

With humble reverence turn aside the hilt,

   Lest some invaluable gem be lost?

Who? why the greater part of this great nation,

Do more or less, feel the infatuation*!

94.

Then think it not impossible that Julie,

   Should in this vision of supreme delight

---

* I once knew a lady (whether akin to the *Pythian Prophetess* or not, is a matter of doubt) who could augur *great* things from the peculiar *cocking of a magpie's tail*!—and now, even as of yore —" Sæpe sinistra cavâ prædixit ab ilice cornix."—VIRG.

Yield up, not merely plate and jewels coolly,

 But all that came unluckily in sight:

The Saints oft blest her, and 'mongst other things,

Promis'd to send a splendid pair of *wings!*

95.

Poor Julie! very little had she need

 Of wings; alas! Imagination's bore her

Too far beyond her altitude; indeed,

 But *few* e'er soar'd so loftily before her!

Yet that there may be some, who've wing'd as high,

I fancy, 'tis not many will deny.

96.

Folly will not be limited, or madness,

 And I imagine, carried to excess;

It yields a melancholy sort of gladness,

 That tortures half—and half perhaps may bless:

But *then* destroy th' illusion,—all is ended,

And fancy's long lov'd light, with night's deep gloom is

  blended.

97.

For, when the dearest hopes, that warm the heart

 In youth enkindled, and in age awake;

Twin'd with the very soul of all thou art,

    Fade—why the heart itself, perforce must break ;

Snap, like a high-stretch'd lutestring, and the tone,

No more resembles, what we once have known !

98.

And such the lot of her, who so believ'd,

    Returning reason dawn'd—but not to save ;

Enough to point the phantom that deceiv'd ;

    Then sunk—like lamps hid in the damp cold grave !

Yet left's the tale ; I've tagg'd a moral to it,

Because the ladies—" *like a moral poet*.*"

---

   * I have taken this, I confess, upon *report ;* but, I trust, I am circulating no *libel !*

TO

THE WHOLE RACE

OF

Critics

TERRESTRIAL OR OTHERWISE,

THESE COME GREETING.

————

CRITICS, ye're cross old Gentlemen, I'm told—
    And most prodigiously delight in snubbing:
Permit me just to make a little bold,
    And thank ye *not* to pickle me a drubbing;
Or—(tho' I don't suppose he *will* forsake ye)
I may sincerely wish, " The Devil take ye!"

Yet, in the name of wonder, Noble Crits!
    What could he make of ye with all this hasting?
Ah me! I fear, to turn his cursed spits,
    And give poor scribbling folks a hearty *basting.*
Farewell! be merciful; and tho' but men,
I'll dream you're angels, nay—*arch*-angels, then!

Julian.

A FRAGMENT.

What tigre or what other salvage wight,
Is so exceeding furious and fell,
As wrong, when it hath aim'd itselfe with might?
Not fit 'mongst men that do with reason mel,
But 'mongst wilde beasts and salvage woods to dwell.

Faerie Queene.

𝔍𝔲𝔩𝔦𝔞𝔫.

A FRAGMENT.

I.

Heard ye the tramp of steeds in yonder glen?
Mark'd ye the squadron, winding down the steep?
Tho' the still hour of midnight, thou may'st ken
The stern array of death; who soon shall sweep
That host away,—and scarce an eye will weep
The wrack he leaves behind.   Where heroes trod,
Where heroes died, the husbandman shall reap,
And heedless trample on the hallow'd sod,
That hides from human eye, the image of a God!

E

II.

But say; in night's dim veil, why horsemen throng,

Cautiously must'ring in yon gloomy dell?

Cheer'd not by trumpet, rous'd not by the song

That wakes the soul of war? No martial swell

Echoes along; silent as by a spell

Onward they move:—and hark! that loud alarm,

Now do they play the part of cowards well;

By heav'n! they fly, the dastards spurn the palm

That aye should firm the heart, and nerve the warrior's

       arm '

III.

Yet such they seem not:—and in sooth, again

Embattled re-appear, the scatter'd troop!

What means that hasty course along the plain,

The shrill halloo, and wide resounding whoop?

Perhaps some foe, pursues the timid group,

Or they but feign to fly,—then wait the attack!

Like the fierce vulture, ere with fearful swoop,

She pounce upon her victim's feather'd back,

Hov'ring, she hangs awhile, then cleaves the airy

       track.

IV.

And such their fate! behind a jutting rock

They skulk: the adverse bands make head,

Rush unprepar'd—and sink beneath the shock!

Where is their once presumptuous boasting sped?

Life, honour, all—in one sad moment fled!

Deem'd they forsooth, that warriors would submit

Without one struggle? Not thus wolves have bled,

Not thus, the steed is broken to the bit,—

And shall proud man alone, stoop as proud man thinks

    fit?

V.

Stoop! oh! 'tis grating to the meanest ear—

Think then, how galling to a soul of pride,

A fiery heart, submission loth to bear,

Or stem th' impetuous flow of passion's tide :—

And such the heart of him, who now did ride

Heading the victor troop; 'twas he first drew

With sinewy arm, the sabre from his side;

And, as his glance, caught its ensanguin'd hue,

His vengeful soul beat high, and on the warrior flew.

VI.

Thou—that ambition's treacherous heights would
    dare,

And madly tempt the dangers of its way;

The rock thy grasp, will loosen,—yet beware

For if it fall, no pow'er its force can stay!

'Twas to ambition, Julian, fell a prey.

The noble proud Lord Julian; once he rose

As the young eagle, springs to meet the day,

But scaling heav'n, ere yet that day had close,

His weary pinions sunk, the scorn of haughty foes.

VII.

It boots not to unfold, his fortunes past,

The pow'r that dragg'd him downward; 'tis enough

He fell—and like the tempest riven mast,

Crush'd all beneath him: Tho' the shock was rough,

His callous soul, but spurn'd the fierce rebuff,

On blood he rose, nor dropt one pitying tear!

Alas! ambition, should be sterner stuff;

Compassion, vainly looks for refuge there,

In whose dark wild domain, she ever finds a bier!

VIII.

Beneath a larch-crown'd mountain's haughty brow,

Where stand the ruins of an ancient pile,

He and his followers fled—sole refuge now '

Proudly magnificent it once did smile,

Tho' now the ivy creep along the aisle,

And its decaying pillars scarce support

The tott'ring tow'rs.   But a little while,

And thou shalt mourn its lofty honours brought

To nothing: nothing! lo, it is already nought!

IX.

In its dilapidated halls, the jay

And rook, hoarse screaming, seem to Fancy's

    eye,

To mourn the ravages of Time's dread sway,

And o'er its ashes croak the funeral cry.

There, if the roving hunter chance to pry,

Or to secure his prize, the robber wight,

Redoubled clamours fill the vaulted sky—

Then wheeling round and round, in airy flight,

Pitch on the ruin'd tow'r, or in the field alight.

X.

By scenes of mirth and joyous pastime, caught

Haply of yore, gay triflers flutter'd here,

Sporting till loath'd satiety had wrought

The death of sense, and clos'd the mad career ·

E'en then did beauty turn a willing ear

To him who breath'd the adulating strain;

And still, to heart of woman, what so dear?

Ah me! how seldom hath it breath'd in vain—

The ear the Serpent charm'd, what charm shall free

    again?

XI.

But my Muse wanders from her beaten track,

To what *might* haply be.   What was, what is,

Should now demand her song.   The mighty wrack

Of ages, is as nothing : present bliss

And present woe weigh heavy, and to this

The heart of man is thrall; except the few

Who desp'rately dash down life's precipice,

Careless of all; to them, the fond adieu

Of hearts enchain'd by love, assumes no sadd'ning hue.

XII.

To them the sigh **of** hope, the trickling tear,

That wars with nature in the human heart,

That should speak grief—yet is joy's harbinger,

From whence dear pleasures, long untasted, start

Back into life—to them no care impart!

But wherefore linger?   To that Chief I turn,

Whose hopes defeat but nourish'd, tho' the smart

Of ruin'd fortunes, made his proud soul burn

With a still, smother'd fire, like embers in the urn

*   *   *

*   *   *   *

*   *   *   *

*   *   *   *

XIII.

High birth, and lofty hopes, were Julian's; never

So fair a blossom met the sun's warm ray;

The blast of pride came—blighted it for ever,

And his dark soul no more beheld the day!

Yet it was great—'twas form'd for greatness; they

Who first its dawn had witness'd, deem'd it bright

As ever beam'd in boyhood's young essay;

But when to man it ripened!—Oh let night

Hide, in her densest shroud, the awful truth from

    sight!

XIV.

Fell he alone?   'Mid iron solitude
Was there not one who cheer'd the lingering hours,
And calm'd his spirit's haught, impatient mood,
By spells all mighty? scatter'd a few flow'rs
Upon his dreary way?   In gloomy bow'rs
Few enter, ay *but* few with gentle care
Warm the cold heart, that feels the deadening pow'rs
Of a long train of ills.   They come not there
Where the lone couch is press'd by sick'ning wan
     despair.

XV.

But he *had* one; one comforter, who shed
The meed of pity, tho' he claim'd it not,
Whose fortune, fame—whose heart for him had bled,
Had deeply bled!   Could *this* be all forgot?
Ill-fated Laura, may the hand that shot
The poison'd arrow in thy youthful breast,
So fond and so devoted!   May his lot
Be still to seek, in vain to seek, for rest;
A mark for shudd'ring man, to point at, and detest!

*　　　*　　　　　　　　*

*　　　*　　　*

*　　　*　　　*

*　　　*　　　*

XVI.

Her fair arm rested on the mossy stone,
And her dark tresses floated in the gale,
That thro' the ruin pour'd a gentle moan,
Like the soft sigh of sympathy, the tale
Of sorrow draws!　　　*

*

XVII.

*　　　　*　　　　*

*　　　　　　*　　　　*

Thro' the flow'ry vale
(Flow'ry no more), war's clamorous voice was heard,
And Julian, triumph'd in the bitter wail
Of widows, and of orphans; but the word
" Destroy," rose up a prayer of vengeance to heav'n's
　　Lord!

XVIII.

And now, yon bloody standard, in the eye
Of his ambitious hopes, wav'd far and wide,
Blazing in all the pomp of victory!
Again his soul, soaring on wings of pride
Savagely pour'd along the furious tide,

Of war, and crime, and horror; o'er his head
His beamy falchion, waving, fell to hide
Its brightness, but in death's dark sheath;—it sped
Like the strong lightning flash, vindictive, fierce and red.

XIX.

On, on he flew; thro' the impetuous fray,

The straining eye scarce follows where his might,

Swept down th' opposing host, whose fair array

· Now broken, sunk beneath the blast, and flight

Starting, on phrenzied wing, forsook the fight.

But this the fate alone, where Julian fought

Desp'rately brave: not far upon the right

An aged warrior toil'd; nor he untaught

To guide the strength of war, with glorious trophies

    fraught.

XX.

Unspent the vigour of that arm, tho' time

And sorrow's keener pow'r, its force assail'd,

And had perchance impair'd; yet many a clime

Its mightiness had felt: the lofty quail'd

Before it; direly the oppressor wail'd,

Its patriot indignation!—In decay

Amid the battle's fury, it prevail'd,

And thrice, had turu'd the fortune of that day,

Which mighty wrongs provok'd—-wrongs blood alone

    could pay!

XXI.

Julian, enraged, beheld the squadron yield,

To that bold leader, and his martial few;

" Dastards," he shouted, and the blood stain'd field

Echoed the sound; full well his warriors knew

Its fearful tone, and to th' attack they flew:

'Twere better to sustain the whirling blade

Of death itself, than the proud chieftain view

In his dark mood.   Something unearthly play'd,

In that full eye's stern glance,—they felt it, and obey'd!

XXII.

Fiercely he rush'd along, where 'mid the shock

Of adverse hosts, the aged warrior fought,

Still unsubdued:—'Gainst a projecting rock

Wounded he stood at bay, by toil and draught

O'erpower'd, yet firm; until his keen eye caught

The flash of vengeance there: then swiftly sunk

Their clashing sabres.   Rapidly as thought

Stroke follows stroke, till Julian's weapon drunk

The valiant heart's best blood, and reeling, fell the

trunk!

*   *

*   *

*   *   *

*   *

XXIII.

Where the tall sycamore, and graceful ash

Drink the cool freshness of the summer stream,

The lost one, sorrow'd.   Like a meteor flash

Across the firmament, had been the dream

Of youthful fancy ! oh ! so bright the beam,

So glorious too,—her soul had caught its flame

To burn, nor be extinguish'd : the dear theme

That dy'd her cheek in blushes of sweet shame,

And bade her bright eyes glow,—was Julian's morning

    fame !

XXIV.

Wealth may attract, and titles oft allure

The female soul, but Laura, felt the glow

Of a devoted heart, as bright, as pure,

When glory twin'd her wreath around the brow,

Of him she lov'd ;—alas ! how darken'd now

The light of her young hopes ;—and such shall be

Thy fate, who mak'st thine idol, and dost bow

Before th' ignoble shrine, a patient knee—

Ay, such shall be thy fate, then weep, weep bitterly'

XXV.

'Twas evening, and the stars sparkling above

Diffus'd their radiance round.   The time gone by,

And those dear hours of extacy, when love

So sweetly shone, return'd,—but as the eye

Of thought shot thro' the past, the chilling sigh

Of agony arose.   Her father left

'Mid life's dark woes, to feel the misery

A thankless child prepar'd him ! Oh this cleft

Her erring heart in twain, of joy, of hope bereft.

XXVI.

The lone lorn tear, crept down her pallid cheek,

Wrench'd from its frozen souree ! In bitterness

Too exquisite to tell, she vow'd to wreak

Curses oh her undoer ; — to redress

Her sorrows, and her wrongs, (whose fierce excess

Destroy'd her youthful excellence)—and die !

But her heart *could* not curse him,—it could bless,

Twas made for blessing, tho' the scornful eye

Of him, who won the gem, regardless pass'd it by '

*   *   *   *

*   *   *   *

*   *   *   *

*   *   *

XXVII.

" What! whining still fond thing? those eyes should
 " shoot

 " Love's burning fires,—thou quenchest them *chaste*
 " *maid,*

 " No more on't pr'ythee, touch thy magic lute,

 " And charm some wand'ring sylphid to thy aid!"

In covert scorn he spoke ; trembling, dismay'd

Vainly she strove : " Cease, cease, the jarring strain,

 " Poor melancholy fool, when I am laid

 " Deep in the grave's dark nothingness ; again

 " Weep, if thou lov'st it so—I hate thy sick'ning plain!

XXVIII.

 " To night I'll pledge thee, and thou too shalt quaff,

 " From such a glorious bowl, the sparkling wine

 " That it will sparkle brighter ; and the laugh

 " Of merriment bid that dull soul of thine

 " Leap in a glad delirium! Barnardine,

 " Give me the bowl of victory,—there pour

 " The vine's rich juice ; 'tis heav'n to hearts like mine!"

His henchman came,—a *skull, yet warm* he bore,

Thro' whose long hoary locks, drop'd mingled wine and
 gore!

XXIX.

Flash'd the dark eye of Laura, as he held

Malignantly exulting to her lip

The tomb's foul spoil, which shudd'ring she repell'd:

" So my coy fair one, thou disdain'st to sip

" The proffer'd blessing ; 'tis a goodly scrip

" Of eloquence however, nor e'er yet

" Spoke it so soundly ; 'tis the very tip

" Of orat'ry ! come drink, and thou'lt forget

" List'ning to its soft strain, thy heart's foreboding

       threat."

XXX.

Loathing, she turn'd away.—" Drink Laura, drink,

" And thou shalt yet hear more—*much* more ;

" Thy wanton soul, why start? would scarcely think,

" This gorgeous canopy, contain'd the store

" Of—*brains*, would'st term them ?—that did subtly

       pour

" Immeasurable ruin on *my* head!

" Kneel to it gentle Laura, and adore

" Its mightiness ! Oh may his earthy bed

" Be an immortal curse—such, such as *I* would spread !"

XXXI.

Had'st thou beheld the phrenzied staring eye,

That Laura, darted at th' infernal chief,

It would have palsied thy young frame! the sigh

That follow'd too, was horrible,—belief

Staggers in her wild flight: it was a grief,

That thou may'st *feel*, not *tell!* Madly she spoke,

" My father, oh! my father!"—as a leaf

Drops, blasted from its withered branch, the stroke

Came o'er her shatter'd soul, and the worn heartstring

     broke!

XXXII.

Her dull glaz'd eyeball, on the chief was turn'd

In all death's gloomy terror: then, *but* then,

His haughty spirit consciously burn'd

'Mid the decay of nature!

*   *   *   *

*   *   *   *

*　　　　　　　　　　　　　*

*　　　　*　　　　*　　　　*

*

*　　　　　　　　　　　　　*

XXXIII.

" Father, a tale of anguish thou hast heard,

" But I have *felt* it—oh how deeply felt '

" Curs'd be those honors, for they but conferr'd

" The misery I endure and must.　Impell'd

" By pride and fell ambition, I have held

" N y steady course along—a noxious star,

" Shedding its baneful influence ;　I've swell'd

" The stream of desolation ;　pour'd afar

" The thirsty scourge of fate, thro' all the ranks of

war !

XXXIV.

" I won—I trampled on the loveliest flow'r

" That ever blossom'd, near the lonely cell;

" I might have sav'd it from the winter's pow'r,

" But demons bade me, and it fell—it fell!

' For this I suffer all the pains of hell,

" For this my soul burns, deathless it must burn,

" And know no healing! When I'm dead thou'lt tell

" My woeful story,—bid the stranger turn

" From the proud Julian's hopes—to his unhonor'd urn!"

DR. MAC SAP;

OR,

𝕿𝖍𝖊 𝕱𝖆𝖑𝖑𝖊𝖓 𝕾𝖙𝖆𝖗.

———————

A TALE.

———————

His mountain back mote well be said
To measure height against his head,
    And lift itself above;
Yet, spite of all that nature did,
To make his uncouth form forbid
    This creature dar'd to love!

PARNELL.

DR. MAC SAP,

———

I.

"OH Love! what a sly little urchin art thou!"
    Hath often been sung, by sweet bards, male and fe-
        male,
Who sigh'd as they felt thee, they could not tell how,
    Heaving the heart, like a bark that we see sail;
Tumbled and tost by the wild waves of ocean,
    Ready to sink at one moment, and then,
As if it had taken a brisk working potion,
    Rapidly shoot up to heav'n again!
Such thou art, Love, say the songs and the singers;
    And if it be true, what a turbulent lad;
Good heav'n, no wonder that wisdom should bring us
    Strait jackets, and bid us be chain'd up for mad;

Should curse all thy witcheries ; spurn at thy wiles;

And like gold on a coffin, see death in thy smiles!

2.

For me, tho' the bells of gay folly should sound,

And the cap (so delightful to most!) should be found

Adorning *my* head ; I so doat on thy charms,

Little Love! I must live—ay, and die in thy arms.

Why wisdom may frown ; let her rail if she will,

To the last ebb of life, I'm thy votary still,

Whilst loving and lov'd; let who will head her cries ;

I'll tell her 'tis folly—'tis base to be wise !

3.

But wisdom may fall down the precipice too,

In pursuit of a brilliant cameleon hue ;

May feel (the fine sneers of its excellence past)

'Tis caught by a vapour—a nothing, at last ;

And will raise large pretensions to folly, as soon

As another, and cry like a child for the moon !

'Tis then that we laugh, loudly vulgarly laugh,

At the vast erudition that made him a calf ;

Then proudly we crow o'er the arrogant elves,

That deeming us mad—prove the madmen themselves.

4.

Doctor M'Sap was a man of some breeding;

O'er Scotia's bleak regions there liv'd not a wight,

For learning so fam'd—of such wonderful reading,

As he of whom now I've the honour to write!

He was—and re-echo it, all ye fair vallies,

Ye mountains sublime, with your snow-cover'd tops,

Throw, throw the proud tidings as far as that wall is

Where the bright flaming bound of the universe stops;

He was, so profoundly immers'd amid sines,

'Mid co-sines and tangents—'mid Greek too, and

Latin—

So vers'd in the *sound* of Falernian wines—

That oh! if the carcase, like minds, we could fatten,

It had never been his, I will venture to say,

To have slept upon *sounds* at the close of the day;

To have dreamt o'er a page of Horatian treats,

Or guess how a hog nicely **barbecu'd** eats:

No, no; he'd have **gorg'd** a brave supper, instead

Of wind in his stomach, and froth in his head!

5.

Yet learning he had; and ('tis fit the world **know it)**

On each fair **occasion** could learnedly show it.

Argumentum absurdo, he grew such a dab in,

He forc'd the proud parson to quit his mud cabin,

To acknowledge that *he* had, as well as my lord,

No right to be equally mad and absurd!

Nay, such was his wit, his wise lordship would yield,

And the birch-wielding pedant decamp from the field;

Who left him at length, in the midst of despair,

To find the tenth part in the breadth of a hair!

6.

With a mind so celestial, so brilliantly wrought,

  'Twas just, that its case should be excellent too;

Twas just, that the dome of the palace of thought

  Should be bright as the rays of the sun shining thro'

But, alas! how perverse is Dame Fortune to man,

  How sparing of gifts, and how futile to beck them ·

If pockets be given—so saving her plan—

  She often denies a few shillings to deck them!

7.

Dr. Mac Sap had a visage whose leanness,

Had little been worn by his efforts of cleanness;

He judg'd, and most soundly,—whatever is spare,

Has little about it, that should not be there:—

He judg'd, and could prove it, with infinite stress,

Whatever is small, has small need to be less,—

And *ergo*, his lean and lank features should not,

Lose one little atom of all they had got!

But added to this, (you'll believe it, I hope),

It sav'd him a wonderful fortune in soap;

And—(whilst I am yet, on the topic of saving),

Prevented expences enormous in shaving;

Because like a plaster, it cover'd the chin,

And nourish'd his beard on the dainties within.

Then his person, as chronicles tell—(be they true)

Was as lank as his face, and as *beautiful* too;

As tall as a May-pole, I'd certainly say,

But a hump on his back, took the tallness away;

His legs were like pins, when inverted, and you,

If it please, may suppose, that each head was a
          shoe;—

Tho' his foot, to adhere to the truth, was as large

As, compar'd with its mast, is the keel of a barge!

8.

Ay, wisdom may fall, I have said it, and mark

What fate had decreed to this gay letter'd spark.

9.

Embosom'd in woods, of the growth of an age,

    Tradition says, stood the magnificent house

Where Lord Donald dwelt, when the season bade wage

    Dread war on the ptarnigan, moorcock and grouse.

His lordship was now in the downhill of life,

And had known all the plagues of a termagant wife;

All the moments of fretfulness incident to one,

And he hourly regretted the moment he knew one!

She govern'd his " *lordship*," and paid him the rent

In coin that a miser had anxiously spent,

Had lavish'd profusely around him, and giv'n

The bountiful donor, a portion in heav'n!

One morning the chase having tempted to roam,

Ere evening clos'd in, he turu'd wearily home;

But alas! no dear thought of its comforts arose,

For home was to him, not a home of repose!

All was bustle, and seem'd a huge chaos of strife,

As he tremblingly ask'd for my lady, his wife :—

" She's dead"—was the answer; " what dead!" my lord

      cried

" Good Stephen inform me, how was it she died ?"

" As a christain should!"—" Ah ! what pleasure to find

" Thro' life she had ever the *cross* in her mind :

" Did she bear it with firmness ?" "Oh firmly, my
    lord."

" Ay, ay, I believe it, still firm to her word,

" ' *I will*,' was the rule of her conduct thro' life ;

" But she's dead—and her lord is at peace with his
    wife!"

Oh happy the heart, that finds peace once again,

    Who can welcome the dove that had wander'd astray!

And no longer oppress'd by the conjugal chain,

    His lordship pass'd gaily life's desolate way.

10.

Sweeter pledges of love, then remain'd to Lord Donald

    No eye ever witness'd—no heart ever lov'd !—

" *Twa bonnie Scotch lassies*:"—but Matilda, the one
    call'd ;—

That 'mid all the mazes of loveliness rov'd ;

A light fragile form, where the soul's ardent play,

    Buoy'd up by high spirits, was never at rest—

Like that soft, ever changeable, beautiful ray

    Of the gem*, whose pure splendour shed light on a
    breast

---

* The Opal—remarkable for i.s diversity of colour.

As warm as 'twas innocent—gentle as gay

From which hearts that had feeling turn'd never away,

But would glow, as her eyes beam'd that magical thrill,

Which governs the soul in despite of the will.

Then, if moments of anger, gave birth to a frown,

The smile that *still* follow'd was heav'nlier grown;

And the heart far more happy in tasting of this,

Than all the pure radiance of unalloy'd bliss.

For it was not the frowning, 'tis torture to hide,

More pain to one's self, than all others beside!

Not that hell of ill-humour, that deadens each grace,

And pictures the heart in the gloom of the face!

No, no; 'twas the breeze that culls sweets from the throng

Of the flow'rets it woos, as it passes along;—

'Twas the clouds in a heav'n of beauty, that throw

O'er the contrast, a brighter, a heav'nlier glow.

Oh! ever she shone—whether smiling or grave,

New charms but succeeded, like wave upon wave;

Like an exquisite lute, touch its chords as you will,

Ev'ry tone that it yields must be exquisite still!

11.

Such, such was Matilda; and who then can blame

The omniscient Mac Sap, if a terrible flame

From her bright eyes enkindled, first sing'd ev'ry part,

(As ye singe a wild goose), and then blaz'd round his heart;

That heart, which till thrown in this dreadful quandary,

Had repell'd all the charms of his kitchen-wench Mary;

That heart so courageous, that ne'er before thought

Of love—save in learning, or saving a groat;

Now sad and perplex'd, and consuming to boot,

Look'd wan like a lover, and sigh'd to a lute;

Perhaps the " *Scotch fiddle*," had better been nam'd—

But then I, and the Muse, and the Doctor were sham'd;

For *lutes* 'mong poetical lovers, you know,

Are the essence of elegance now—all the go!

12.

Matilda, who sometimes bestow'd, as she pass'd,

   A nod, or a smile, in return for his bow,

'Mid mirth and astonishment found out at last,

   What a conquest adorn'd her invincible brow;

What glory she'd won, over Greek verbs and Latin,

Now love amid learning had tumbled so pat in!

13.

But the Doctor discover'd, his " dignified ease"

Had lost all its charms, and no longer could please;

F 5

And what, alas! what could he do?   Should he call?

Ah me! he could summon no courage at all;

Still this love of his ev'ry way tortur'd him so,

Each varied expedient but varied his woe!

They tell me that love is a rose among thorns :

   And *one* poor opinion no axiom unsettles,

Or I'd boldly declare, tho' each oracle scorns—

   That love is a full-blooming rose among nettles!

Which grasp as you ought, like a sage man of mettle,

And then, forsooth, where is the sting of the nettle?

After *all*, should she scorn, from love's touches exempt,

Throw back on the coy one the glance of contempt;

Let the scorn of thy heart in each eye be pourtray'd,

That ever should follow the insolent maid :

Thus ever act bravely, in courtship or marriage,

And nine points to ten, you avoid a miscarriage* !

14.

Long waver'd the Doctor; this—that way he steer'd;

Rejecting one plan, as another appear'd;

---

* " Brisk confidence the best with woman copes "

Childe Harold.

Till at last (and oh ! genius, how greatly dost thou
Shine eminent e'en from no beautiful brow—
How proudly thou lookedst from him that I sing of,
When his excellent thoughts, like to jackdaws a string of,
That in order arrang'd, swing about in the air—
Came tossing and tumbling brilliantly there!)
He resolv'd a magnanimous note to compose,
And call the fair lady, the " Summer's best Rose ;"
For he oft had been told, that a rose and a lily
Would make up a cheek for Elysium ; and still he
Knew the laws of the Ancients, regarding the fair,
Gave them ample permission to seat themselves there ;
Besides, as a lover, what less could he do,
Than at once be polite and poetical too ?

15.

Now he fumbled his books, and he conn'd ev'ry phrase,
That might throw the young heart of the maid in amaze;
That might force her submission to th' wonderful scholar,
   Who knew ev'ry word's derivation and kind ;
And for him, like a spaniel, wear love's glassy collar ;
   For him, leave the halls of her fathers behind!
He wrote, and he alter'd—then alter'd again ;
'Twas now in too harsh, now too florid a strain ;

Till at length, having labour'd a day and a night,
A safe accouchement gave the following to light :

16.

THE DOCTOR'S EPISTLE.

SWEET ROSE OF THE SUMMER !

                              Thine eyes' intense glory
  Hath dazzled my soul ; and so sweet is thy fame,
That if thou'lt affect me, hereafter in story,
  With mine, future ages shall couple thy name.

Think, think ! when the Genius of History, rising
  With her light-beaming pencil, shall scribble my life
In stateliest phrases—how sweetly surprising
  That—" Dr. Mac Sap took Matilda to wife !"

Yes, yes ; but my keen mathematical senses
  This love hath so dull'd—so encumber'd my breast,
That mechanics can't leave me, with dull moods and
      tenses,
  Is my sweet adolescence, abstracted from rest.

Algebraïcal reasonings die as they're born,

    In the cloud that engender'd 'em.—Euclid himself,

Alack! hath been view'd with unmerited scorn,

    Bespangled with cobwebs that cover my shelf.

My ventiduct's stop'd—scarce a breath is embowel'd;

    Oh! virgin, in effumability, I

Shall be quickly diffus'd, if my wounds are not now

        heal'd

    With the balm that exudes from thy dulcified eye.

Nunc vale et vive: this heart's oscillation

    Can thine alone guard from a fearful mishap;

And oh! how lucif'rous will be the ovation,

    The resuscitation of

                    SANDY MAC SAP.

17.

A little gossoon, in a rude tatter'd coat,

Was dispatch'd to the fair, with the erudite note,

Repeatedly caution'd to act circumspectly,

And deliver the embassy charg'd with correctly;

While for fear of omission, the diffident lover

Bade the boy tell his messages over and over;

Sent him off; then recall'd him, again and again—
Re-repeating, each time, the bewildering strain,
Till at length, as he thought, being fit for discharge,
Twang'd the string—and the arrow flew straight to the
      targe!

18.

From a flight such as this, 'tis but fair to suppose,
Ere long he beheld Summer's favourite Rose;
When, making a bow with astonishing grace,
  (For in truth he had practis'd a fortnight before,
As the Doctor believ'd it a requisite case,
  To be able to *bend** to the fair you adore!)
I say, having bow'd to the lady, he took
From his old ragged pocket a time-shatter'd book,
Which the Doctor presented, to keep the note clean,
And fit to be touch'd by the hand of a queen!
'Twas a grammar, he said, and an emblem to prove
That his heart was the worn tatter'd grammar of love;
But which, if she pleas'd to accept of—oh Venus!
That heart would be happy, and gay, and serene as

---

    * Hence, doubtless, his " *hump*" arose!

The bee, whose loud music exultingly greets
The flow'ret it rifles of virginal sweets!

19.

Ceas'd the lad; but his accents, so piercingly shrill,
On the organ of hearing reverberate still.

20.

Could I picture the fairest expression of charms,
  The bright-laughing eye, and the dimpling chin,
Where the soul's animation the dull heart alarms,
  And a smile of applause from the Stoic can win—
By heav'n! 'twere nothing to that which now shone
In this light of the North—in this loveliest one!
'Twas a mirth like rich blossoms, gay, varied, and free,
That adorn, in its *season*, the promising tree;
'Twas a mirth, from which spleen could recoil not--a
        thing
Whose charms, in malevolence, deaden'd the sting;
With a wit, whose refinement, a brilliancy gave
To the forms it reflected, like stars in the wave;
And graces, which not all the flourish of schools,
All the airs affectation bestows on her fools,

Can impart : no, not one single ray,

Round Fashion's mad votaries, ever will play :

It was Nature's own workmanship, purest and sweetest,

   Of all that in woman approacheth divine ;

'Twas that something unknown—but with which if thou

     meetest,

   Oh treasure it up, in thy heart's inmost shrine ;

'Tis a spell will preserve thee, thro' life make thee blest,

And gild thy dark tomb, when thou sinkest to rest !

21.

But yet she was woman—after all. but a woman,

   And sarcastical gaiety rules more than *one* breast ;

Coquetry perhaps is a word, that's more common,

   And better describes the idea of a conquest !

And Matilda resisted not, could not resist,

   The pleasure arising from such a flirtation ;

A thing far too tempting by maids to be miss'd,

   Especially fools, the delightful occasion !

So the lad with his trappings, all flutt'ring in air,

Was bade to await the commands of the fair,

Who with arch smiling countenance, took up a pen,

And scribbled these lines, to " The wisest of Men."

22.

THE REPLY.

To him, on whose visage sage learning hath written
  The art to subdue the most prudish and coy—
May a young blushing maiden confess herself smitten—
  Confess how she doats on her wise Highland boy?

Oh! thou, erudition's profoundest support,
  Whom wealth or nobility ne'er could bewilder—
Fly, fly on the wings of impatience to court,
  To glad the sad heart of thy anxious

MATILDA

23.

All the transports of Dr. Mac Sap I must leave,
Kind reader, for thee, and thy fancy to weave;
For if thou hast past thro' a similar fate,
Thou wilt forcibly feel what I cannot relate;
Wilt confess with a sigh, even short as it seems;
And dream tho' it be—'tis the sweetest of dreams!

24.

" Fly, fly," said the lady; and he had obey'd
  · Her commands to a tittle, if will, altho' good,

Necessity had not unhappily stay'd,

 And bade him, by no means—do more than he could.

For wings he had none ; and what worse is, indeed,

He had not so much as the tail of a steed.

And truly, ill-luck must that lover betide,

Where will and necessity sadly divide!

A dreadful dilemma it is, let me tell ye,

And happy, if never such evil befel ye;

But happier far—oh, there cannot be a doubt of it,

If in it, you meet with a way to get out of it !

And the Doctor remember'd, his miller would lend

A steed with delight, to so learned a friend!

Thus far it was well ; and he quickly prepares,

With scissars to lop the superfluous hairs,

Which (if memory serve me aright) you have heard,

His chin proudly nourish'd—a king of a beard !

25.

But now, let me haste to equip him, complete,

And fix him on horseback, confirm'd in his seat.

26.

Reports have prevail'd, that long us'd to the dirt,

He found inconvenience in changing his shirt;

M oreover, (and let it not modesty shock,

One whole one, alas! being the whole of his stock* !)

When the dirt became plentiful—pr'ythee, don't flout it—

Like a man of much sapience, he travell'd without it;

Now, this anchorite shirt had been mended, and wash'd

With the very best mint water, lavishly dash'd,

And plaited so neatly, it beggar'd the skill

Of the whole tribe of washers to brighten the frill;

To make it, in short, more delightfully sweet,

Or to fold it in any one form so complete!

27.

When such was its exquisite plight, only think,—

  Gentle reader, vouchsafe my petition to heed;

From the chain of thy thoughts just to separate a link,

  And say, if it were not hard-hearted indeed,

To break up its purity, sully its whiteness,

  As dark clouds envelope the face of the moon,

---

* The caution of the present day may presume to doubt the
veracity of our record; but on consulting D'Herbelot (Biblio-
theque Orientale), it will be found, " That the potent Caliph
Omar Ben Abdalaziz himself had only *one* shirt; and in an age
of luxury, his annual expense was no more than two drachms!"

And hide from the regions of earth all its brightness,

    Which erst had appear'd with the splendour of noon;

Oh! yes, if thou felt'st but one half what the Doctor

    On this sad occasion, combin'd to distress,

Thou hadst gone to thy lady, altho' it had shock'd her,

    To view thy broad shoulders in nudity's dress!

Thou hadst gone—and if sticks o'er those shoulders were

        laid,

Might'st have shewn unreservedly " *marks of a maid!* "

28.

Let the block strike his skull—nought appears—for

        nought's in it—

Your heads that have wit, haul it out, in a minute;

And our lover, determin'd with no little force

As he slipt on his jacket and mounted his horse,

To bear in his hand, this supreme among linen,

As the only sure way to preserve it from sinning—

From catching the evil, the proverb displays,

" Ill company teaches the purest ill ways,"

Till he reach a snug avenue, leading to th' hall,

Where his body, once more, might submit to its thrall;

And present to the nose of his lady, a savour

That would help not a little, in raising her favour,

And ensure a reception, more flatt'ring than 'twould,

When the warmth of the weather excited his blood ;

And " the white and round pearls," (as the poets ex-

  press)

In pretty large quantities roll'd on his dress !

29.

So thought—and so done. Upon horseback now rear'd,

The ladder-like form of the doctor appear'd,

Half alarm'd, as the horse trotted briskly along,

Provok'd at the ceaseless sharp touch of the thong

Of the whip, which the rider, unskilfully held

In fancied importance prodigiously swell'd !

30.

Boast not of thy knowledge, unfortunate wight,

All learning is useless, if learn'd not aright ;

If it tells thee not, gives thee not, sense to perceive,

The absurdities, madnesses, folly must weave ;

The mark of derision to each sotted elf,

Who can feel not in thee, the true semblance of self;

But with fine air of candour, still cries, " on my word

" I lament that my friend so and so's so absurd !"

Whilst his friend, with as equally candid an air,

Exclaims—" so and so's a great fool I declare !"

31.

Well ! let the world wag as it will, there must be,

Some perhaps that laugh with, more than laugh against

     me ;

And it matters not much ! Is your neighbour a calf ?

Another will think it of you, and the laugh,

The proud laugh of scorn, curls the lip and defies

The warm heart of friendship, that shrinks at its lies !

Then friendship believes, and we see *it* in turn

Tormented, tormenting ;—and fatally learn

That Just as the pique of the moment arises

The heart of the man, or reveres or despises !

32.

To return to the doctor ; behold him approach,

    Uncas'd on his steed, and about to slip on

The bright spotless shirt, when the whirl of a coach

    Disturb'd in his grazing, the spirited son

Of a spirited sire ; what his name, what his race

It is needless to mention perhaps in this place,

And I know not indeed; but the miller, don't doubt it,

Will satisfy those, who are anxious about it!

Suffice it, the steed in a frolicksome mood,

Or offended at those who had dar'd to intrude;

On the new fashion'd toilette of him who bestrode,

His proud back as he leizurely pac'd on the road:

With a bound that set all at defiance, flew past,

Whilst the rider, imagin'd that moment his last;

His immaculate shirt—his antique copper coat,

The delicate kerchief, that twin'd round his throat;

His hat, wig, and—whip, that he'd borrow'd alack;

All, all fled their master, ne'er more to come back ·

Never more to hebold the bald pate, naked brawn,

Of him like a swallow, now skimming the lawn.

33.

No longer erect, see his head on the mane,

And his legs moving backward—then forward again;

While his hands firmly clench'd round the neck of the
      steed,

In vain strove to check the excess of his speed,

As he past by the house, where—(oh shame to relate!)

Stood the bright laughing fair one beholding his fate;

Who begg'd him to stop, while with no little force,

The doctor oft beg'd the same thing of his horse:

And vow'd, and protested with many a groan,

If but once he escap'd he'd leave courting alone ; '

Or at least adore one, who'd more care for his nouse,

And would come and be courted at home, in his house !

34.

The waves of a river that skirted the lawn,

And cherish'd the flow'rets its brink that adorn

Flow'd nigh ;—and the steed unoppos'd gallop'd down,

    When the Doctor, who more than his danger perceiv'd,

Thinking better to break e'en a neck, than to drown,

    Jump'd off, and the horse of his burden bereav'd;

On the soft mossy turf, all his learning was laid,

Somewhat bruis'd, it is true—but less hurt than afraid.

35.

Now troops of fair handmaids all anxiously flew,

To be told of the tumult, and talk of it too ;

And wonder, and reason, as women *will* do

Of all that they knew not, and all that they knew '

And when the denudated doctor, they saw,

They chat'er'd, and blush'd, and re-echoed—" oh law !"

(As to blushes, 'tis proper to add, that some *could* not,

And perhaps if they could, it is probable, *would* not!)

Then back again flew, (like young birds from the chaff,

When they've peck'd all the grain out) with laugh after

    laugh.

36.

But ceasing at length, for e'en laughter must cease,

And the mirth-heaving bosom, sink gently to peace ;

My lord bade his train, healing unguents provide,

For the woful result, that attended the ride ;

To cloth him, and feed him, and fill high the bowl,

    With the heart warming eloquent juice of the vine;

Till the ills of the morning, should die on his soul,

    And the bright wreath of joy again playfully twine ·

Till the love that yet faintly illumin'd his heart

From its ashes, with double the splendour should start!

37.

They say that love sinks, 'neath the goblet's eclipse !

    But they err, widely err, who such faith will maintain,

Stol'n glances are sweet—sweet the pressure of lips ;

    But he wets his gay wings in that fount, and again,

G

With a far bolder flight up to happiness soars,

And around, all the charm of his witchery pours !

Oh ! say not the bowl, is the grave of the boy,

  'Tis a sparkling beam of a rapture that is

Like the dream of a Saint, when the world's base

     alloy

  Hath fled, and the soul drinks a foretaste of bliss !

38.

Ay, the doctor soon felt all the warmth it inspires,

  All his troubles forgot, and but love now alive ;

With a look of proud consciousness oft he inquires

  When the Lady Matilda, might haply arrive.

Delay on delay, put his patience to trial,

  Till the shades of the ev'ning envelop'd the sky,

And then to himself, he protested denial

  Should hold him, no more from the flash of her eye.

39.

And now he discerns, (with what joy let those say,

Who themselves have been tortur'd by fearful delay) ;

He discerns a fair maid, with a curtsy of grace

And a look, scarce repelling the smile from her face ;

Who beg'd he'd obligingly honour her lady,

    With a short *tête-à-tête*, where she then would con-
        duct ;

With gladness renew'd, altho' greatly afraid, he

    His breeches and courage resolvedly pluck'd !

40.

Now with heart, that would fain have been joyous, —ad-
       vanc'd he,

And in spite of his bruises right merrily danc'd he;

Till he reach'd the saloon, where the lady awaited :

    Oh then how that heart beat about, pit-a-pat!

He open'd the door, and with glee so elated,

    Fell headlong (unfortunate man!) o'er the mat;

Why runs not the lady to help up her lover?

    Why stands she, like marble dejectedly there?

Oh say, did not modesty wisely behove her

    Of *false steps*, and man's cunning arts to beware?

He rose; still she mov'd not! Sweet maiden, the gloom

With her thick flowing veil, hath now darken'd the
    room,

It needs not to him, thou ador'st, be so coy;

Oh speak to him, mute, and bewitch him with joy!

41.

'Tis silence around, and how sadly ye stand,

Ye lovers, as touch'd by some magical wand!

Rouse Dr. Mac Sap, all your courage arouse,

Think no more, think no more, of the whys and the

    hows.

'Tis bravery wins all the beauteous and fair,

And 'tis this must alone win that excellence there!

42.

" Miss—Lady Matilda," the doctor began.

    Not a sound, not a decimal part of a word,

Gave the wish'd for response, to this desperate man,

    Who had spoken, so much, to the child of a Lord!

What now shall he do? He had heard 'twas a rule

    'Mongst the fair, that dull silence, gives hearty consent;

And heard, the short time he had been in love's school,

    'Twixt lovers, a kiss was a pleasing event!

Such boldness was horror; but then, did he not,

    Offence might be giv'n, tho' he hardly knew how;

So unus'd to the art, he had almost forgot,

    If perform'd on the nose, on the lip, or the brow!

What must be done, *must* be, who is there can doubt it?

    The doctor himself, altho' giv'n to distrust,

Would allow a self-evident truth had about it,

 A something that even uncertainty must

Yield up without contest—so no other book did,

Demonstrate its truth, but that sage fellow Euclid.

43.

Well, the " *must*" being allow'd him the *how* follows

 next :

And oh! what great men, have small matters perplext;

Some yield up their fame, to one error political,

And lovers their bliss, in a moment, as critical!

One unfortunate " *point*," unprovided for, starts

(Tho' doctors say, form'd nor of " *greatness or parts**;")

And o'erwhelms in the maze it created, the learning,

That pompously boasted, of nicely discerning;

And proves, without wisdom, or logical skill,

Good sense is victoriously eminent still!

44.

But some way Necessity wills him ; the Fair

Unmov'd and in silence, dejectedly there

---

 * " *A point* is that which hath no parts, or which hath no mag-
nitude."—*Definitions.*

Seem'd to hope his advance; (at least so, I suppose,

For the fair seldom love to be far from their beaux;)

And at last, after long evolutions of thought,

His contemplative mood, into action was brought!

" Oh! Virgin, I come!" with deliberate pace

He gravely stalk'd up to that sweet bashful face;

Then extending his lips to their utmost extent,

And with wonderful force, a loud sigh giving vent,

He rush'd to th' attack! But oh! earth, sea and skies,

There came from the maiden's mouth, nostril and eyes,

A black liquid ocean, that spirting outright,

Shot direct in the doctor's large organs of sight!

45.

Oh! Heav'n! what sounds from this lover arose,

As the water, in floods, trickled down from his nose;

As it forc'd itself channels in many a place,

And mark'd with fair streaks his magnificent face!

Oh Heav'n! how echoed the roof with his cries,

As the puddle, in floods, trickled into his eyes!

Rage swell'd his big heart; in a fury he flew,

And—(ill luck betide thee, oh doctor!) o'erthrew

That kind loving maid; but he shar'd the disgrace,

And prostrate reolin'd, 'mid the gloom of the place!

46.

Now burst in upon them, resplendent as noon,

(Or, since it is eve, we will mention—the moon !)

The black and the blue, and the soft hazel eye,

While loud peels of laughter exultingly fly ;

And around the poor culprit, the mirth-loving throng,

(As asham'd and crest fallen, he yet lay along),

Buz like moths round a half wasted taper at night,

That haply escape from the blaze of its light.

47.

But worse the confusion, his senses possess'd,

When he found, oh! ye gods! 'twas a puppet he'd
   prest ;

'Twas a puppet drest up, like my lady, which he

Had mistaken, for that, he so wish'd it to be ;

And he saw but too clearly, tho' hard to believe,

That a man of his learning, young maids could de-
   ceive ;

That a man of his great mathematical skill,

Was no match for a woman ; and bitterer still,

The thought that his name, would be handed about,

The scorn of each ignorant, mischievous lout !

48.

Oh! worlds would he give, to escape from the string

That mock his disaster, and jeeringly fling,

Condolement of sorrows, those eyes must bespeak,

That could thus have bedew'd his magnanimous cheek!

'Twas too much, 'twas too cutting for even the one

Whose vanity bade him, be practis'd upon ;

So wildly enraged, without utt'ring a word,

He fled from their taunts—from the house of my lord;

With many an excellent vow, in his wrath

To hate all the sex, as the snake in his path ;

To fly, as the greatest of pests that invade,

A frolicksome horse, and a frolicksome maid.

𝕺𝖒𝖆𝖗

AN EASTERN TALE.

This is the state of Man; to-day he puts forth
The tender leaves of Hope ; to-morrow blossoms,
And bears his blushing honors, thick upon him :
The third day, comes a frost, a killing frost,
And,—when he thinks, good easy man, full surely
His greatness is a ripening,—nips his root,
And then he falls, as I do.

SHAKSPEARE's HEN. VIII.

Omar

—◆—

Auream quisquis mediocritatem
Diligit, tutus caret obsoleti
Sordibus tecti, caret invidenda
Sobrius aula.

Hor.

—◆—

" Oн ! be but humble, and thou shalt be happy,

" Nor writhe beneath the heart-consuming pangs

" That rack th' ambitious soul; and tho' thy days

" Pass not along, in undisturb'd repose,

" Nor all thy nights be tranquil,—(for such bliss

" To hope were vain !) yet happiness may be !"

Thus spoke the hoary sage of Aubukabis*,

And soft as music, floating o'er a hill

* A mountain to the east of Mecca.

Wafted by summer's breath, upon a vale
Of flow'ry sweets,—fell all the words of wisdom,
On Omar's listening ear; and so they sunk,
Calming his troubled soul: " It is, my son,
" The lot of some to climb the trackless paths
" Cf fortune's adverse steep, adverse indeed
" When most she favours ! vigorous they ascend
" Of toil, of danger, and of death regardless,
" And furiously push on : how few succeed,
" To touch the envied glitter ! Say they do,
" Say ev'ry hope completed ; even so,
" View that emaciated frame, fatigue
       And dread anxieties of ill, have worn
" To a poor atomy.   Oh ! wilt thou then
" Dream still ? wouldst thou then seize the splendid
       bowl,
" And quaff its nectar'd poison ? Go, my son,
       Be wise, and to her heav'nly arms, True Bliss
" Shall woo thee !"

                    Thou hast seen
The dark cloud big with waters, whilst a glory
Bright and ineffable, around its edge
From the departing sun, shone forth ; and seen

When his wide glaiing orb had disappear'd,

That cloud wax cold and colder! Omar so

Felt all the warm impression fade away,

As his eye, follow'd up, the lessening form

Of wisdom's reverend counsellor: in sooth

To list that soft persuasive tongue, to mark

The whiten'd blossoms of the grave, that fell

Adown his aged temples, all unmov'd,

Were not to be a man ; and Omar's heart

Yielded due credence, but could yield no more.

He, was as a rock, down which the cataract

Leaps thund'ring, but whose indurated bed

Long laughs defiance at the falling mass !

" The prophet's will be done," the youth exclaim'd,

And forward trod, whilst ever and anon,

He thus held dangerous commune with his heart:

" Shall I ingloriously my day consume,

" Life's little day, nor trace the path to heav'n !

" Thou err'st old man ; thy subtle spell-fraught tongue

" Speaks falsely ! Can it be th' all righteous will

" To light up fires, that must annihilate

" The creatuies he has made ? Would he have giv'n

" Aspiring thoughts, nor will'd me to aspire,

" Or willing, desolate all hope of bliss

" When prov'd ? old man, it cannot be !"

   So murmuring he sped, and ere the eve

Mournfully turn'd her dark and tearful eye,

On the world's hated throng ; high minarets

And tow'rs of holy Mecca, dimly seen,

Like visionary forms amid the gloom

Rose on his wavering sight.   Here turban'd heads

Of many a dye, mov'd variously along,

Like gaudy flow'rets scatter'd by the storm ·

And there, the bright ey'd beauties of the east

Within their rosy tinctur'd veils conceal'd,

Started along his path ; while oft the sound

Of golden bells, that gracefully adorn

The beauteous neck of Love's devoted fair

(Whose long voluptuous lashes, shaded not

The eye of fire, beneath), floated around,

And in the breeze of Even, died away.

   Omar pass'd on, unheeding thro' the crowd,

And as unheeded ! little thought, the gay

And busy world, bestows upon the brow

Of sadness and of care ; e'en Azrael comes
Unnoted ; still the long loud laugh
Of merriment goes on, and like the ocean foam—
One bubble bursts, and others still succeed !

Amurath,

Now reign'd, the dark destroying Amurath,
And Omar his vizier : 'twere long to tell
The acts of blood and horror that o'er ran
The kingdom of the prophet ! The dire lists
Of death swell'd hourly, and the people's cry
By force suppress'd, now broke out, like a stream
That bursts its flood banks, and o'erwhelms the hope
Of a fair harvest's promise ! Omar saw
The threatening storm, and shunn'd its violence,
Fav'ring the rebel powr's—himself the first,
The mightiest ! It may be, the wan form
Of his enfeebled country, first inspir'd
His soul to vengeance for her wrongs ; but thence,
Thence sprang a latent cause, that darkly twining,
Hung like the adder, and instill'd its poison
In his unquiet breast : he was ambitious,
And when the step from nothing to a throne—
From the slave subject, to the despot king,

Appear'd so safe and easy; then arose

Black thoughts, that spoke forsooth of damning crimes,

But so gilt o'er by sophistry's deceit,

They proudly glitter'd in the borrow'd forms

Of justice and of peace! " Yes, he must die,

" And mine too, let it be from death's cold hand

" To snatch the wreath of popular applause!

" Ay, then shall I be honor'd, and 'tis meet;—

" Who risks the greatest, *should* receive the most '

" But if I fail—the prophet's will be done,

" 'Tis he inspires me, and it must be right,

" 'Tis he inspires me, and I must be bless'd!"

Thus he; and ah! how many have believ'd

The will of passion is the will of God,

And cali'd their fond imaginings divine!

How many maddened dreamers there exist

Who wander o'er destruction's flow'ry paths,

And deem heav'n's hand directs them on the way '

The golden chain that binds us, is so fine,

So subtly wove, the soul in slavery dwells,

Yet fancies she is free!

Uproar, and that wild anarchy, that founds

Her mig'itness on horror, ruled the day,

And night escap'd not the infectious touch :

Now thro' the royal halls of Amurath,

Loose mirth's inebriated form had sunk

Like the expiring taper's ray—loathsome

And darkly flashing, till at length extinct

The gloom and still of night, assum'd again

Their melancholy sway : cloth'd in the hue

Of living death, the trembling anxious Omar

(Himself, commission'd harbinger of death!)

Bent his reluctant, and yet eager steps

In cautious silence, thro' long corridors

And rooms of regal state : The guard, remov'd,

Presented free access to his fell hopes :

But to his soul, the solemn warning voice

Of conscience, yet alive, spoke audibly.

It whisper'd, murderer, inhuman murderer;

It bade remembrance, tell of days gone by,

Of Omar, rais'd to glory—honor'd, lov'd,

By him he would destroy; and then it rung

Ingratitude, black base ingratitude :

Like spirits muttering o'er a grave! appall'd

He shrunk before the monitor, but yet

Turn'd not away : ah! no, the blood stain'd wreath,

Ambition, twines around her votary's soul,
Is as indissoluble, as the links
Of Fate's eternal will,—and 'tis as hard
For mortal strength to break !

Onward he pass'd, with that determin'd fear
Which cowards have assum'd amid despair,
And so, done boldly: but He never knew,
Until this darken'd hour, the withering blast
Guilt spreads upon the soul, and till this hour
His heart had been undaunted. He had brav'd
War, in ten thousand rugged shapes, but ne'er
Felt half the horrors of a scene like this !

The tyrant slumber'd o'er the gilded couch,
Breathing last eve's debauch. His very rest
Perturb'd and fearful; whilst a dreary smile
Play'd with such ghastliness upon his brow
As had affrighted horror, and excell'd
His deepest, phrenzied mood! The eye-balls sunk
And fixt on air, inanimately dim,
Mock'd living nature, and bequeath'd to death,
More terror, than he brought!

                    Still Omar gaz'd,
Fearfully gaz'd, upon that awful sight,
And half forbore the stroke ; but now to turn
Argued a weakness, which his soul despis'd.
Died he or not, the morrow must display
Rebellion's crimson'd banner, streaming round,
And one—as he, ambitious of a throne,
Usurp dominion, and to death consign
The envied favourite of a tyrant lord !
Here, hesitation ceas'd ; the sparkling blade
Descended, whirling thro' the gloom of night,
And dy'd its lustre in that heart, the chill
Of inhumanity had frozen o'er.
The black blood slowly trickled, and a groan,
One agonizing groan, rung the sad knell
Of his unwept decay, while death's dark angel
Bore from a gladden'd world, the evil one
That troubled all its peace !

                    Hark, oh hark !
Heardst thou, but now, a deep drawn bitter sigh
That seem'd to rend in twain, the o'er-fraught breast
It sprang from ? Was it fancy all ? again
It meets the ear, and Omar trembling stands,
And awe-struck ! there, there, the shadowy drapery

Shakes,—tho' without the breeze hath died away,

And not a leaf's in motion ! Sure some pow'r

Hastes to avenge the bloody massacre,

And hurl the fated thunder at that form,

So pale and tremulous ! One busy moment

Rife with despair like this ! Oh ! it had arm'd

Against divinity his impious hand :

He would have struck—(so hopeless seem'd his fate!)

Tho' pregnant with eternity of woe !

With a strange savage laughter, he uprais'd

An unstain'd sabre, that had grac'd his side

But on high days of festival, (such day

The last bright morning smil'd on) nor ere yet

Had drank red slaughter, from the rapid tide

Of all o'erwhelming war.   Fiercely it fell

Where the sad sounds had utterance, and blood

Warm human blood, from the pure spring of life

Follow'd the blow ; a fearful, deathly shriek

Succeeded, as convulsively there rush'd

To his scarce conscious ken, a beauteous form,

Like the struck dove from the entangled brake,

Wet with her own heart's blood : her tresses hung

In wild disorder, o'er a brow, that shone

With a pale sickly lustre, but e'en so

In excellence unrivall'd ! wildly too

Eyes that once beam'd but tenderness, and seem'd
Image of love's divinity, to which
All hearts were sacrific'd ; and whose bright flame
Consum'd the offering, but new splendour shot
O'er the pure altar's holiness! how dim
How darkling now, and oh! could virtue say
Its purity was still, still undefil'd ?

A groan of anguish from the bleeding fair
Gave back to Omar's soul, the fleeting sense,
And drove the filmy darkness from his eye:
He look'd—again, and dreadfully he look'd
On this young lovely one.   Oh! could it be?
Was it a vision that he saw, and what
Its monstrous import ? In a madd'ning voice
Loud, and as terrible as his, the fiend*,
Whose fearful tones, on the last awful day,
Will rouse the sinner from his mould'ring tomb
He spake: " Woman, who—what art thou ?"
A sigh of deepest bitterness was all,
All his foreboding heart had need! It was

* Monker.

(And fate could curse no deadlier,) the one,

The chosen one, in whom all life, all love,

That warm'd his youthful bosom, was concenter'd;

'Twas his own darling Zara ; she, for whom

He first but dream'd of honor, and for whom

He woo'd the name of regicide! Now, now

He felt ingratitude's severest sting—

A damned one's torments, for he felt them just!

Hell hath no fire more terrible than that   *

Which burns the trusting heart, betray'd to death

By all it lov'd the dearest, and he, too

Of harsh experience, tried the bitter fruit!

True, Amurath was a tyrant, and he died

A tyrant's death ; but 'twas not thine to kill—

Not thine, ungrateful traitor !   He who shed

The early dew upon the springing flow'r,

And beam'd bright rays of sunshine, merited

No such return!   Thou feel'st it now, indeed,

Heavily, heavily—one dark hour too late!

Oh ! the decrees of heav'n are wondrous ; they rise

Amid intensest darkness ; but the flash

Of Justice strikes the unexpecting world,

And thro' its dread magnificence appears

The hand of the Omnipotent!   Then swells
The vengeful storm of Fate; the guilty then
May tremble, for they feel, and they confess,
The Lord is God, and mighty to destroy!

That bitter drop, on Omar's woe-blanch'd cheek,
Bespeaks his fearful agony of heart:
Zara, the fall'n Zara, beauteous still,
E'en amid guilt and death, clasp'd his cold knees,
Upholding scarce their burden ; whilst her eye
(That eye, whose ever-varying glance, his soul
Once rapturously hail'd, now turn'd
Dim 'mid the damps of death!) sought mercy yet;
Not in warm hope of life—for that was past,
Fleeting like guilty dreams : " Canst thou forgive
" A wretch like me ?"—at intervals, she said,
Gasping for breath—whilst ev'ry passing word
Struck like a dagger, the lorn heart of Omar ;
" Canst thou forgive th' enormity of wrong
" I've done to thee ?   Didst thou but know the toils
" That won me to destruction, thou wouldst pity,
" And then, perhaps, wouldst pardon one so lost!
" But I could never tell thee all—'tis too,
" Too terrible, and conscience—oh! it burns,

" It maddens me; more deadly pangs lie *there*,

" Than all thy dooming sabre can inflict

" On this adulterous breast!   Omar, dear Omar,

" I die—but do not curse me; Alla then

" May pardon – *thee !*"   The wings of Azrael,

Striking the midnight air, were heard afar;

And as her spirit fled, the angel's breath

Chill'd the warm fount of life, and Zara sunk

A pallid corse, in that red shroud of blood!

The verdant branch, by gentle force essay'd,

May bend unbroke; but suddenly constrain'd

From nature's course, it spurns the rude assault,

And snapping—fades for ever on the stem !

Thus died the lofty hopes ambition rais'd—

Thus sunk into decay the aspiring Omar ;

Whose busy mind, weigh'd by unforeseen,

Unthought of evil—could sustain no more;

And the pure ray that lights the human frame,

That spark of heav'n's own fire, expir'd; and there

A pitiable darkness cover'd all.

What ill, what punishment can man endure,

So terrible to poor humanity, as is

The wrack of intellect? oh! it is bitter;
And bitterly it shews the weaknesses,
The nothingness of man; it bids him look
With less presumption to the Lord of all—
To Him who gives—to Him who takes away '

Now Omar rush'd impetuously along,
Back from the hall of death, in safety led
By the sure guidance of the Prophet's arm!
No sound escap'd him; but his wild eye shone
With all the glare of madness.   Having pass'd
Unseen the confines of the Haram wall,
He hurried on, fleet as the antelope
Bounds o'er the flow'ry turf, when the loud cry
Of her pursuers mingles with the breeze;
So on, throughout the city's lonely paths,
Unchalleng'd.

Borne by some secret impulse,
O'er the wide champaign rapidly he sped,
And ere the morning ripen'd in the east,
A lofty mountain rear'd its stately head,
Stretching along his way.   Wearied he fell
Beside a rugged cave's dark aperture,

H

And sleep, sweet comforter! in magic spell
Enwrapp'd his shatter'd soul!

  " Father of mercies! let thy servant bend
" His knee in thankfulness, to Thee that gave—
" That giv'st him life and being!   Man in vain
" Would be, if thy directing providence
" Pointed not out the realm of future bliss,
" And bade him win it!   Holy Alla, this,
" And *this* alone, proves thy beneficence
" To man, fall'n creature! and for this is due
" (And ah! how little worthy of thy name!)
" His warmest pray'rs and praises!"

  Thus, in the purest fervency of soul,
The sage of Aubukabis pour'd to heav'n
His morning orisons, and thankfully
Bless'd Alla and his Prophet, who had shed
The calm of Virtue o'er his blameless heart!

  Now, from his rocky habitation see
The holy man step slowly forth, to hail
The bright sun's rising majesty, and mark
In the magnificent and peerless works

That overspread creation, the all-wise,

All-beauteous law of the Supreme Creator.

Why starts he now? and why, with uprais'd hands,

And tremulous, so sadly sighs? Ah! there

Lies the wild haggard countenance of one

He dearly lov'd—the sleeping, madden'd Omar.

He wakes, he wakes—and oh! how horrible

To see the vacant roll of those large eyes

That once shot lightnings o'er his manly frame,

When war's shrill voice stirr'd up his soul to arms!

With sudden spring,

Shouting, he rush'd precipitately past,

And scal'd a massy rock, that beetling hung

O'er the wide waste beneath: no transient pause

Upon its verge, gave one short breath to horror!

A dreary howl, loud and long, and fiend-like,

Fled from his bleeding body, as he leap'd

Headlong adown the steep; while his sad soul

Left its dark tomb, to meet the just decree

Of an offended and almighty Judge!

The sage beheld the woeful scene of death

With many a heart-felt pang, and pitying tears

Wet, with their kindly dew, his furrow'd cheek.

Much had he lov'd the youth ; and could grave counsel

Have turn'd the fiery bent of passion's law,

Omar had yet liv'd happy—yet belov'd !

But vain th' attempt to fertilize a soil

Nature forbade to flourish ; vain th' attempt

To ripen fruits 'mid winter's chilling sky !

MISCELLANEA.

" Spissis indigna theatris
" Scripta pudet recitare, et nugis addere pondus."

HOR.

FROM ANACREON.

ΕΙΣ ΕΡΩΤΑ.

WRETCHED indeed, is that man's fate,
  Whose heart obdurate cannot know
What joys on love sincere await,
  Or taste the " luxury of woe !"

And he who feels love's poison'd dart
  Glide swiftly thro' his trembling frame,
And feels it rankling at his heart,
  The term of " *wretched*," too may claim.

But ah ! can words express the pains
  Of him who loves to love's excess,
When not one single hope remains
  To blunt the keenness of distress ?

FROM THE GREEK.

She sang—and Philomela mute,
　With envy heard the rival strain,
And then, as if to dare dispute,
　Began to trill her notes again!

Soon ceas'd the lay ; in deep despair,
　To find her own sweet sounds surpass'd,
She sunk, exhausted, on my fair,
　And on her bosom breath'd her last!

October, 1816,

TO KATE.

—

Nay, call me not fickle, altho', dearest Kate,
  My heart at this moment is ranging,
For it flies to repose on thy bosom its fate,
  But there it remaineth *unchanging* !

Yet wilt thou receive it?   Oh kindly comply;
  It shall shield from thy heart ev'ry sorrow;
And the tear that to-day may have moisten'd thine **eye,**
  Shall be dried by its warmth ere to-morrow.

October, 1816.

THE QUARREL.

—

TALK on, fair maid, I'll calmly hear thee—
    I'll keep my temper in despite;
But if thou deemst that I shall fear thee,
    In sooth, thou art mistaken quite.
The man who fancies by assuaging,
    To bend a woman to his will,
Like oil pour'd on the ocean raging,
    Will only find—it rages still!

No, no; besides, I *like* the roaring,
    I *like* to see huge waves arise;
Now down upon the sea-beach pouring,
    Then re-ascending, touch the skies:

I love to hear thee scolding, sweet! too,
    To see those orbs of sparkling flame;
To view thee stamp thy little feet too—
    It proves thou'st *eyes*, and art not *lame* !

What! nay pry'thee do not cease, love,
    So *grand*, thy little angers are;
We will not sink so soon to peace, love,
    Indeed, we've hardly *tasted* war;
And,—sullen now! well, that's a change too,
    Variety is pleasing still;
Tho' thou'rt lovely, I can range too,
    Feel, perhaps a warmer thrill!

Ay, ope the window, strong winds blowing
    May drive that dark cloud from thy brow;—
E'en as I thought, the smile is growing,
    And sunshine, will appear just now!
Not so, by heav'n! the clouds are breaking,
    And tears in copious show'rs descend;
Thy grief, my stubborn heart partaking,
    Here *feign'd* indifference must end.

Why do you weep ? I love you dearly
   There's not on earth, a heart so true
That loves so fondly—so sincerely ;
   Or would more gladly bleed for you !
Dear Mira, no ; then but one kiss love,
   Sweet pledge of peace, ne'er tried in vain
For thrilling hearts, know most of bliss, love,
   When anger, yields to love again.

Nov. 1816.

ANACREONTIQUE.

———

Away with all sadness,

In grief there is madness—

Why should we hearken to sorrow and care ?

Fill, fill the thirsty bowl ;

Let ev'ry joyous soul,

Pledge, till he drain ev'ry drop that be there.

'Twill add a new vigour,

'Twill soften the rigour ;

The storms of adversity waken, alas !

As the clouds, dropping rain,

Give a beauty again,

To the flow'rets all faded, and withering grass.

Then shun ev'ry sorrow

Think not of the morrow,

Old Time's done sufficient to *mellow* our wine,—

If the rogue dare appear,

To admonish us here,

We'll drown him, by Jove! in the nectar divine.

Jan. 1817.

HAPPINESS.

" Nos procul expulsos, communia gaudia fallunt."

OVID.

IN search of happiness, man flies,
Each scheme, and each expedient tries.
   All, all alas! how vain!
And what, altho' he labour hard,
Too often is the sole reward?
   Pain—agonizing pain.

Thus children thro' a thorny brake,
Rush with extended arms to take,
   The warbler's downy bed:
The pointed thorns, the way oppose,
They wound their flesh, they tear their clothes;
   But all they sought,—is fled!

May, 1817.

ALTERED FROM CATULLUS.

———

SHE vow'd she lov'd me, dearly lov'd—
And I believ'd her true, as fair;
But oh! my broken heart has prov'd
She wrote with water—on the air'

May, 1817.

———

EPIGRAM.

———

I LOVE devotedly, where most I hate;
Ask ye the meaning of a thing so new?
Alas! I know not,—'tis the curse of fate,
To feel it torment, yet to love it too!

TO CLARA.

—

GIVE me a thousand kisses, sweet,
The thousand kisses, oh! repeat ;
Repeat them, dearest, o'er and o'er ;
Repeat them till thou hast no more!
Thus whilst thy lips of *weight* are eas'd,
The heart of malice will be pleas'd,
And envy too, will be content,
When all thy gifts of love are spent.
So each some profit finds in this—
Then kiss my dear, begin to kiss.

June, 1817.

* " Da mi basia mille, deinde centum," &c.

CATULLUS, Lib. I. Car. 5.

TO MIRA.

———

Come, Mira! let us seek the bow'r,
  Where roses bud, and woodbines twine,
Enjoy at least, one happy hour,
  Nor thus at destiny repine.

For ah! it but augments our woe,
  And whilst time moves with tardy wing,
'Tis hope alone, can bid joy flow,
  And happiness mid sorrow spring.

Then pr'ythee, be no longer sad;
  Sing, sing that mournful song again,
Which once had pow'r, would *now* it had
  To dull the keenest thought of pain!

Nay, look not thus, for oh! 'tis hard

   To watch that sorrowing tearful eye,

And yet denied the sweet reward,

   To soothe thy heartfelt misery.

Yet sing, yet sing; for who can tell

   When angels catch the heav'nly strain,

Obedient to thy magic spell,

   E'en happiness may come again !

October, **1817.**

ON WOMEN.

(FROM CHAUCER.)

———

Thıs world, alas ! is full of guile,
   And all, as onward they proceed,
Will often find the sunbright smile
   Is not a sunbright smile indeed !
   Woman alone, alone can plead,
Free from deceit, and form'd to bless,
   Yet somewhere, have I chanc'd to read,
" Beware, beware of doubleness !"

How fresh and gay, are summer flow'rs,
   The white and red, the blue and green ,
But soon the blast of wınter pours,
   Destroying what so fair hath been !

Thus change in ev'ry thing is seen,
But *not* in woman, all confess,
And yet it is but right I ween,
To warn you against doubleness.

The pallid orb of night appears,
Often array'd in silvery hue,
And oft a face of darkness wears,
Changing each rolling month anew;
And who duration ever knew?
What can the fickle pow'r repress?
But woman is—oh! ever true,
Yet *still* beware of doubleness!

The bright and lovely summer's day,
The sun's effulgent cheering pow'r,
As night approaches, die away,
And leave the dark and silent hour;
O'er all inconstancy doth tow'r,
And learned men have said no less,
But woman, truly all that know her,
Know her free from doubleness!

The billow, that the high rock laves,
   And proudly threats, will soon again,
Retreat, and mix its foamy waves
   With the calm'd waters of the main ;
   How fair the day, yet heavy rain
Descends, and proves all fickleness;
   But who of woman, can complain,
Devoid of change or doubleness !

November, 1817.

L'ENVOI.

THEN since inconstancy hath been—must be,
O'er all of mortal nature ; were not we
Madmen, nay worse than mad, hoping to find
Constant, the fickliest of a fickle kind ?

December, 1818.

TO MARY.

———

Love, in thine eyes delighted plays,
  And shines, as sparks on di'monds glow,
And oft the wily urchin strays,
  Roving that bosom white as snow !
But, ah ! sweet girl, in time beware,
  Dost thou not know his roguish art !
The little plunderer hides him there,
  To steal thy unsuspecting heart !

June, 1817.

TO ⸺

⸺

My ⸺ dear and hallow'd name,
    How could my Muse so long forget,
To kindle at the purest flame
    That ever burnt to heav'n yet?
Could feel affection's warmth inspire
Nor joyful strike th' enraptur'd lyre!

Forgive—and now perhaps the strain,
    Which votive thus, I wake for thee,
May strengthen the too feeble chain
    That binds the throne of memory;
And bid me sing in sweeter song,
As time shall sweep the chords along.

2

Perhaps too, when the bitter thrill

  Of misery hath pass'd away,

And Peace shall come—(for come it will!)

  And thou shalt hail a happier day;

Then thou wilt hark, no longer sad,

To tales of thy all-rhyming lad.

Wilt thou not? yes; for there's a pow'r

  On Poesy's enchanted ground,

That sheds like some sweet scented flow'r,

  Its perfume over all around;

And ah! tho' some may scorn the gem,

The Poet only pities them '

His soul, has many a rapturous minute,

  Which the cold bosom, cannot know,

That feels no spark electric in it

  Of Poetry's inspiring glow.

Then may he not well pity such,

Insensible to softest touch?

And what, tho' trifling be the lay;

  The bard's creation, rude and wild—

Companion of life's doubtful way,

 He loves it, as a favorite child!

Then think, oh! only think how hard

To blast the day-dreams of the bard.

To blast them, said I? that were vain,

 A foolish—an absurd endeavour,

For wake him, and he'll sleep again

 As sound, ay more enwrapt than ever!

Such happiness can only yield

Fair Poesy's elysian field.

And wonder not, I harp so long

 On such a strain—the dearest, best;

For I must be the child of song

 Till sinks this beating heart to rest:

Whate'er my fate, where'er I roam,

Here, I shall find a peaceful home!

If pleasure's cup, before me glow,

 Which neither fears, nor sorrows dull—

This talisman, will bid it flow

 E'en yet more bright, more beautiful.

As glittering gems, in water thrown,
Give it a lustre, not its own.

But if—ah! sad reverse of fate!
　　Tempests shall rend the shatter'd sail,
The lyre that bless'd my happy state,
　　Shall soothe me, in the boist'rous gale;
And as I mournful touch the string,
Hope, 'mid the dreary wreck will spring.

Farewell! my ———— mayst thou find,
　　This day, and each succeeding one,
Unruffled by the stormy wind,
　　Bright'ning beneath the glowing sun;
And when—retard it heav'u! thy day
Shall sink, oh! be't in peace away.

January, 1818.

TO JOHN ST. M——— ESQ.

———

FLY, fly, my St. M——— from the cares of the soul,
And pledge me to-night, in the eloquent bowl,
Which sparkles as brightly, as if, my dear boy,
The nectar we quaff'd, could partake of our joy ;
As if it too, were anxious, one moment to spare
From that hoary old vagabond, *Dominie* Care !

There are moments, believe it, whose sunshine of bliss,
May prove perhaps, even more transient than this ;
When the blast of Misfortune, with terrible pow'r,
Shall strike the fair bud as it opens to flow'r ;
As it feels the warm glow of the ripening sun,
And we view it decay, when its beauty's begun !
Ay, *here*, when the rod of affliction shall smite,
Farewell—oh farewell ! to the cup of delight ;

No more shall it sparkle before us; no more

Can the dear voice of Friendship, its sweetnesses pour,

Unfelt and unheeded, it passes away;—

As meteor beams, o'er the cold waters play,

You behold their bright forms, in the stilly profound,

But darkness and death, are enveloped around.

 Yet thou, my kind friend! oh never may'st thou

The dark hand of Sorrow, more heavily know,

Than that soft soothing pressure, whose touch will im-

  part

A pain—but a pain, that yields balm to the heart!

Yes! still may the thrill of enjoyment be thine,

And to witness thy happiness, ever be mine;

Be it mine, to exult as thy genius glows,

And warm, as that laurel encircles thy brows,

Which shall form a pure wreath, as unfading and dear

To the Muse that inspires thy young bosom, as e'er

Amid Immortality's temple, was furl'd,

By the glad hand of Fame, to astonish the world?

June, 1818.

TO A FRIEND.

FEAR you the noise of scribbling folk?
   They're harmless all the brood;
Like the young raven's dismal croak
   'Tis but demand for food!

Nor let it aught thy anger raise,
   If crowds admire their strain—
The spark of genius, soon will blaze,
   And prove the slander vain.

But scorn their *praise*, a foolish race
   Love fools! and thou shalt find,
The wreath they twine, a last disgrace,
   To chain the manly mind!

June, 1818.

TO ———

'Οργίζόμενος τω αδελφῶ αὐτοῦ, ΕΙΚΗ, ἐνοχος ἐσται ΤΗ ΚΡΙΣΕΙ·''

Sτ. Matthew, Chap. V. Ver. 22.

" For he'd a way, that many judged polite—
" A cunning dog—he'd fawn before he'd bite."

CRABBE.

Yes, venom'd adders lurk unseen,
    And dart upon their trembling prey;
But thou, dark monster!—thou hast been
    More veil'd, more venomous than they!
Causeless, yet terrible, the hate
Which urged thee calmly to await
A moment big with utter ruin,
And load it with a friend's undoing!

Oh! oft to his deluded eyes,

Thy shallow soul was trick'd in lies;

And oft thy arts rais'd hope of joy,

More deeply, direly, to destroy.

As moon-struck wretches sometimes may

　　Their sorrowing hoping friends deceive

With semblance of returning ray,

　　Whilst subtle lines of death they weave!

Is it not sad, in life's young day,

To view our dearest hopes decay?

And manhood's harp, so newly strung,

　　But vibrate each discordant tone;

Whose chords that should to bliss have rung,

　　Make the cold heart more drear and lone!

And oh! the bitter heartfelt sight,

　　Of cheeks that once could brightly smile,

Turn chill away, their long-lov'd light—

　　The victim of a villain's wile!

Yet I'll not curse thee, wretch!—no, no;

Thy bosom needs no curse to know,

Than that awaken'd conscience brings—
  More poignant than the scorpion's ire;
It bears along ten thousand stings,
  And burns in unconsuming fire!

June, 1818.

TO ——————

(ON BEING PRESENTED WITH "FALCONER' SHIPWRECK.")

———

DEAR Lady, when I read the lay—
  This mournful lay—I'll think of thee;
And pausing often, will I say,
  Does Fanny yet remember me?

And if the flatterer Hope reply,
  " Her feeling heart could not forget"—
Oh! it will stay the bitter sigh
  Of many a sadd'ning fond regret!

'Twill come, like spirit tongues, that breathe
  O'er youthful visions, music's strain—
Whilst Joy her fairy bands shall wreathe
  Around the gloomy couch of pain!

For trust me, tho' I've often sung
   The speaking eye, the pouting lip;
And often too, delighted hung
   O'er extacies too—fleet to sip.

Never in dream, or dreaming song,
   (And oh! this heart might well be calmer!)
Have I believ'd, 'mid life's gay throng,
   A heart—a kinder, or a warmer.

But yet—and thou'lt believe me, Fanny—
   'Tis not thy loveliness—no, no;
Beauty may brighter beam from many,
   Tho' not, in sooth, to charm me so.

It is, it is, the open heart,
   That link'd in friendship's dearest ties,
Bids hallow'd rays of splendour start,
   That kindles in thy laughing eyes.

It is that *something*, which t' impart,
   Words were in vain; and all I know,
'Tis a bright halo, round the heart,
   That lights, that lives but in its glow!

And thou wilt give me Friendship's right—
A right I'll proudly, fondly own;
The thought, that tho' remov'd from sight,
To memory but dearer grown!

Wilt thou not?—yes, I know thou wilt!
And haply if some future day,
Thine eye glance o'er the tale of guilt,
Or love, that marks my lowly lay.

Oh! let it whisper a kind thought
Of him thou never more may'st see;
And Time, whate'er he brings to nought,
Shall never harm—one thought of thee.

October, 1818

TO ———.

———

Can my soul cease to love thee?   Say not so,
Friend of my youth!   Altho' thy sallow cheek
The hectic flushes, and the pulse of woe,
Beats thro' thy care-worn frame, and bids thee seek
The refuge of the grave.   Ah me! how weak
Is man; the frost-work of a winter's morn,
Which the first blast that rudely blows, shall break,
And leave him stript of beauty and forlorn,
For ev'ry passer-by to look upon and scorn '

Once o'er the rest thou wert pre-eminent,
And they to thee as nothings; blended now,
Almost with nothing thou art!   This th' event
Of Fate's harsh edict—to which all must bow,
But who, of all, hath suffer'd more than thou?
Oh! they be few, if any; never yet
Did the young heart with fairer visions glow,
And never did the sun of glory set,
In darker, bitterer hour, or night more sternly threat.

And now thou dost inhale the vital air,

A mockery of man!   Ay, we may smile

'Mid storm and sunshine—happiness and care,

The sweet vicissitude will reconcile :

But thine is all dark cloud—no hopes beguile

Thy long long day ; and tho' the stern arrest

Of Death claim sole dominion—he, the while,

Laughs at thy misery, and denies the rest,

Which shuts the languid eye, and stills the throbbing

       breast !

November, 1818.

SONNET TO TIME.

———

Time! what a peevish wayward thing art thou—
  Now in the rainbow's vivid colours drest,
  Soothing to sweetest peace, the care-worn breast,
And driving clouds from Sorrow's wrinkled brow;
  And now with chilling aspect of despair,
  Destroying the bright buds that flourish'd there,
In all Spring's freshest beauty. Woe is me!
  Oft have I seen thine eyes vindictive flash
  Consuming Hope's young day, and felt the lash,
The scorpion lash of bitterest misery!
  Yet have I known thee too, in fairer hours,
When joy danc'd gaily down the path of life—
  When heav'nly dreams, in Pleasure's fairy bow'rs,
Were more to me than heav'n! but oh! thine ills were
    rife!

August, 1818.

TO LAURA.

Yes! I must love, tho' frowning Fate,
   Darken the ray that brightly shone;
Tho' Youth's gay dreams be desolate,
   And blisses pass untasted on!

Tho' all that warm'd my raptur'd heart,
   When first it beat for love and thee—
Should like the lightning flash depart,
   And leave but vengeful flame for me.

Still must I love—well, fondly love—
   And let the censuring world condemn;
'Twill glad my care-worn heart to prove,
   I lov'd thee more, in hating them!

REMEMBER ME '

TO H——TTE.

———

RE*E*BER me, when fleets the hour
Of bliss, and pleasure's passing flow'r
No more delights thy wearied eye ;
When from thy bosom bursts the sigh,
And tears adown thy pallid cheek,
The agony of fate bespeak ;
When friendship's feigned caresses flee,—
Then, lady, then remember me.

For I would soothe the hour of ill,
And tell thee, there were moments still,
That after all of misery past,
Should wear the face of joy at last :

And I would bid thee hope; and while
Thy cheek put on the timid smile,
I too could joy—for sweet will be
The thought that *then* remembers me.

Yet tho' the smile, thy smiles impart,
Should never reach the sorrowing heart,
(As sunshine on the tomb may rest,
Tho' cold beneath the mould'ring breast!)
Still thou shouldst hold dominion here,
To this fond heart for ever dear ;
And little all the world would be,
If thou, in sooth, rememberest me.

Remember me! oh! wilt thou not?
And must I live, and be forgot?
Must I endure e'en this, and yet
Unable, if I would forget ?
No—tho' that heart, the hallow'd shrine
Where burns this glowing heart of mine,
Reject its incense—there will be
Sometimes a gentle thought of me.

Dear lady, do I err?—the rill
That wanders onward, freely still
Refreshes with its silver spray,
Each flow'ret ere it wends away,
And tho' it pause not, yet will give
The gentle show'r that bids it live!
And lady, thus that thought will be,
The thought that once remembers me.

February, 1819.

TO FANNY.

————

WHERE are now the glad moments of exquisite pleasure
    That gilded life's path with a heav'nly hue?
Oh! long ago faded—but yet the lost treasure
    Can memory's dream of delusion renew.

Resplendently there the dear flow'rets she nourish'd,
    Once more re-illum'd, their wild beauties display;
And again the heart feels as at first, when it flourish'd,
    Ere it bitterly drank of the cup of decay!

Yet, Fanny, those moments, so dear to this bosom,
    So lov'd—I ne'er welcome, ne'er wish their return;
Tho' sweet while they last, 'tis such anguish to lose 'em,
    Hope weeps a farewell from the desolate urn!

Thou pitiest me, Fanny?   If aught could awaken
    A beam of delight o'er a heart chill as mine,
It would be the proud thought, that my grief was partaken
    By a heart so belov'd, and so thrilling as thine.

SONG.

———

Away, far away from the false one ; believe me,

   Death lurks in the wave he will press thee to sip;

He will swear that he loves, and while swearing, deceive

      thee,

   And poison the goblet he holds to thy lip !

Thou hast seen the bright beams of the day-star at morning,

   Thou hast seen all their brilliancy darken'd at noon;

And thus shall thy happiness die 'mid the scorning

   Of him, who so prais'd thy harp's virginal tune !

And then all abandon'd—life's hopes dull and darkling—

   Like the lorn tear, that drops from that lustre-dimm'd eye,

One moment, the sun in its ray saw it sparkling,

   The next, and amid the cold earth it shall lie !

By heav'n ! 'tis madding to think, that with feeling,

   With the warm heart of woman, man ever should play —

From the temple of peace thus insidiously stealing

   The gem of the soul from the shrine where it lay.

     June, 1818.

TO H——TE.

I've seen, with scarce a wish, a sigh,
  The brightest beams of loveliness ;
I've gaz'd upon a dark blue eye,
  Nor felt its magic pow'r to bless !
But then I saw no soul as bright,
  Shine thro' that radiant world of charm ;
And 'tis not brilliant specks of light,
  'Mid the cold atmosphere, that warm.

Ah no ! the flutt'ring vacant throng,
  That pass o'er life's delusive way,
May claim, perhaps, an idle song,
  But cannot light Love's ardent ray.
The blush of gentleness—the thrill
  Of feeling—oh! their pow'r is such,
The heart indignant spurns the will,
  And melts before a single touch.

Then blame not, lady ! if I dare

    To love where *all* I love's combin'd ;

Too soon I saw that thou wert fair ;

    Too soon—thou hadst a fairer mind !

Hopeless, perhaps, I feel the sting ;

    Hopeless, perhaps, I'm doom'd to pine ;

Yet I *will* love the loveliest thing,

    Tho' Heav'n deny that blessing mine !

August, 1818.

SONNET.

WRITTEN BY MOONLIGHT, AMONG THE RUINS OF KIRKSTALL
ABBEY, YORKSHIRE.

———

Amid the mould'ring monuments of Eld.
    With reverential awe inspir'd, I stand.
    Oh! for the stroke of an enchanter's wand,
T' embody all that Fancy hath impell'd
    Upon the straining thought! Youth—age may
       dream
    Touch'd, like the ruin, with the moon's pale beam;
But youth alone feels all the charms that glow,
    With more than real bliss, when calling back
    Things that have been, in the bewildering track
Of ages far gone by! Oh! ye who know
    The world's vain joy—unreal too as this—
Say, can ye deem a happiness more pure
    Thrills thro' the human heart, when from th' abyss
Of misery ye turn—forgetting to endure?

August, 1818.

TO ———

———

YES, there are moments, when the heart
    All that it lov'd, can love no more,
Yet feel again th' envenom'd smart—
    A ray of what it felt before !

And like that transient soften'd flame
    The day-star at his parting throws,
Bright, with a minute's flush, it came,
    Then sunk—ah ! fleetly as it rose.

But could the sun with warming beam,
    Glow thro' the world, yet leave it chill ?
No, tho' this bosom's fev'rish dream
    Is past, yet I will love thee still.

K

Love thee, with all a brother's love—

    And if it be my fated lot,

O'er the dark waste of life to rove,

    By few regarded—or forgot,

For thee (tho' sear'd and blighted fall,

    The hopes that light the youthful breast);

For thee, again, I'll woo them all,

    To bless thee—and thou *shalt* be bless'd !

March.

EPIGRAMS*.

―――――――

" I LOVE thee, Curio," longing Delia cries,
As full on me, she turn'd her goggling eyes;
Spare me—oh! spare me—by the pow'rs above,
Thy love were hate—thy hate, to me were love!

―――――――

* The following are extracted from an unpublished MS. en-
titled, " Sketches from Nature," and which may one day meet
the eye of " *a candid and enlightened public.*"

LITTLE ELEGANCIES.

Hear'st thou yon madam? how her tongue doth roll,

On " little elegancies," bless her soul !

From day to day, her song is still the same,

Still trembles there, the consecrated name ;

O'er all she does—o'er all she means to do,

This phrase, the clust'ring *verbage*, twinkles thro';

Yet spite of all the pains she takes to show it,

Not one alas ! not one in twenty know it!

What then the reason ? not in her it lies,

She's *all* she says: why 'tis the world wants *eyes !*

———

THE TRAVELLER.

Mark that gay sailor :—heavens ! how he talks,

As like a land leviathan, he stalks ;

While little people, such as you, or I,

His knowledge know not, nor his height can spy.

How indeed should we ? None of us have been

Where he has wander'd—seen, what he has seen ;

That often people, who admire his skill,

Applauding tell us —" he is *wand'ring* still !"

THE GENEROUS FRIEND.

" Doubt not my faith! whatever some pretend,

" I will stick to you, to the last, my friend;"

So Quitam said : writs, bailiffs, soon undo him—

Yet Quitam's true, he—*to the last stuck to him* !

C—— boasts his great acquaintance, proudly dwells,

On what this lord, or what that lordling tells!

Think ye 'tis true ? The question we will wave—

A peer *may* be acquainted with a knave !

TO WOMAN.

They say I do not love thee! but I do,

And as I love thee—I would *chasten* too :

For well I know, Perfection's *not* a dream,

And Women might be—ev'ry thing they *seem* !

THE TIPSY FAIR.

" DEAR Dr. Slyboots," cries a would-be saint,

" Support me, oh! support me, or I faint;"

" Miss," says the doctor, "have you had a *call?*"

" Oh! *often*, doctor, catch me, or I fall!"

Her maid displays young madam's saintly case,

But were she silent, view that *radiant* face!

———

LAW's like a two edg'd sword—it cannot miss,

And now it cuts on that side, now on this:

To rush in law, wise men are ever loth,

For, (*cut* on one side) then you're *cut* on both !

———

EXTEMPORE EPITAPH

FOR

MISS ——.

HERE lieth one, who'd all the world could give,

And yet she died—because she could not live !

EPITAPH

ON A LADY OF *NOTORIETY*, BURIED NEAR THE PLACE
SHE INHABITED.

HERE lieth one, they say, she liv'd and died,
And lieth here—where she thro' life hath *lied!*

TO ———.

YES, you are listen'd to, but not believ'd,
For if we trusted, we should be deceiv'd ;
Yet, if you say your meaning's to deceive,
'Tis more than probable, we *shall* believe!

ADVICE TO ———

LAUGH, laugh—nor heed what *other* fools may do,
Laugh you at them, they *can* but laugh at you !

Let Philip call his friends—this lord and t'other—
Lords oft are fools, and fools regard their brother!

———

Seest thou yon red plump cheek and chuckling air,
And think'st aught excellent can harbour there?
Pious, yet most irreverent; with care
Sparing, when very madness 'twas to spare;
Without one generous feeling, tho' he gave,
He lives—a compound both of fool and knave!

———

" Jack, Jack, you drink; give o'er—'tis your undoing!"
" Drink, rat me, drink? you lie—I'm only *going!*"

———

Ned hates a niggard—yet the cautious elf
Has too much wit to quarrel with himself!

FINIS.

BARNARD AND FARLEY,
Skinner-Street, London.

Lightning Source UK Ltd.
Milton Keynes UK
UKOW05f0022131216
289858UK00016B/779/P

9 781333 345136